C000108970

Use Your PC to Explore
Digital Music

Gateway
PRESS™

Notices

Use Your PC to Explore Digital Music
is published by
Gateway, Inc.
14303 Gateway Place
Poway, CA 92064

© 2002 Gateway, Inc.

Version 1.0

ISBN: 1-57729-271-5

DATE: 5-13-02

Printed in the United States of America

Distributed in the United States by Gateway, Inc.

Welcome

From the introduction of Digital Music in Chapter 1 through troubleshooting in Chapter 8, *Use Your PC to Explore Digital Music* provides you with what you need to know to acquire, organize, and enjoy music with your PC. This product is designed to accommodate your learning style, and to make learning easy, interesting, and fun. You can stick to just the bare essentials or learn in greater depth by practicing key skills and applying your new knowledge. Our goal is to show you how technology can enhance your life, provide some fun, and open up new opportunities.

More Than a Book

Use Your PC to Explore Digital Music is more than a book; it is a blended learning system that also includes interactive CD-ROM and Internet presentations and activities. These tools all work together to provide a truly unique learning experience. The book presents technical information in visual, practical, and understandable ways. The CD-ROM extends the book by providing audio, video, and animated visuals of important concepts. Continue learning online by logging on to www.LearnwithGateway.com. The enrollment key provided with this book gives you access to additional content and interactive exercises, as well as reference links, Internet resources, and Frequently Asked Questions (FAQs) with answers. This Web site allows us to keep you updated on rapidly changing information and new software releases.

Classroom Learning

In addition, a hands-on training course is offered. Additional fees may apply. Our classes are ideal solutions for people who want to become knowledgeable and get up and running in just three hours. They provide the opportunity to learn from one of our experienced and friendly instructors and practice important skills with other students. Call 888-852-4821 for enrollment information. One of our representatives will assist you in selecting a time and location that is convenient for you. If applicable, please have your Gateway customer ID and order number ready when you call. Please refer to your Gateway paperwork for this information.

Learning map for
Use Your PC to Explore
Digital Music

This map shows how the elements of the Gateway Learning System work for you. The best of an easy to understand, highly visual book, the Internet and CD-ROM are all brought together to give you a unique and truly enjoyable learning experience. Notice how the interactive CD-ROM and Internet activities extend and complement the chapters in the book. Icons in the book will direct you to each element at the proper time.

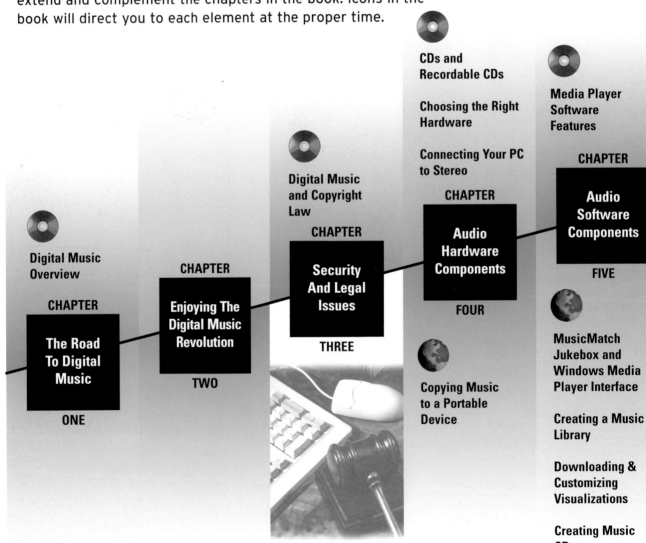

CDs and
Recordable CDs

Choosing the Right
Hardware

Media Player
Software
Features

Connecting Your PC
to Stereo

Digital Music
and Copyright
Law

CHAPTER

**Audio
Software
Components**

CHAPTER

**Audio
Hardware
Components**

FIVE

Digital Music
Overview

CHAPTER

**Security
And Legal
Issues**

FOUR

CHAPTER

CHAPTER

**Enjoying The
Digital Music
Revolution**

THREE

MusicMatch
Jukebox and
Windows Media
Player Interface

**The Road
To Digital
Music**

TWO

Creating a Music
Library

ONE

Copying Music
to a Portable
Device

Downloading &
Customizing
Visualizations

Creating Music
CDs

On Your
CD Rom

 On the
World Wide Web

Downloading
Music Files

Using Media
Libraries

Benefits of
Internet Radio

 CD Burning
Software Features

CHAPTER

Exploring
Music On
The Web

SIX

Sharing Digital
Music

CHAPTER

Recording
Your Own
CDs

SEVEN

CHAPTER

Trouble-
Shooting
Scenarios

EIGHT

 Roxio Easy CD
Creator
Overview

Nero Burning
ROM Overview

Recording
Music

Ripping Tracks

CD Copier

Creating CD
Labels and
Jewel Inserts

You can also take a Gateway class, and this is an ideal way to continue to expand your learning. Gateway instructors are dedicated to working with each individual and answering all your questions. You will be able to talk with other learners, practice important skills, and get off to a quick start. Additional fees may apply. Call 888-852-4821 to enroll. **See you in class!**

Contents

1 The Road to Digital Music 1

Making the Journey from Analog to Digital 2
Reaping the Benefits of Digital Audio....................................8

2 Enjoying the Digital
Music Revolution 15

Recording Digital Music..16
Appreciating Digital Music's Versatility and Portability 18
Finding New Music and Sharing...23

3 Security and Legal Issues................27

Explaining Copyright Law 28
Understanding Copyright Holder Rights............................30
Knowing Your Consumer Rights Under Copyright Law 32
Finding U.S. Copyright Laws 34

Contents

4 Audio Hardware Components 39

Exploring Audio Hardware....................................40
Tuning Into External Audio Devices 53

5 Audio Software Components 61

Understanding Digital Audio Formats 62
Choosing a Digital Music Player..........................67
Using Your Digital Music Player..........................77

6 Exploring Music on the Web 95

Understanding Online Music Formats..................96
Finding Music Online 98
Downloading Digital Music Files 105
Using Online Databases 107
Organizing Your Music......................................110
Exploring Internet Radio 113
Sharing Your Digital Music...............................119
Keeping Your System Secure.............................125

Contents

7 Recording Your Own CDs.................131

Understanding CD Formats and Media...........132
Choosing CD-Recording Software...................137
Recording a CD...139
Creating CD Labels and Jewel Case Inserts 168

8 Troubleshooting Scenarios 175

Resolving Internet-Connection Problems 176
Troubleshooting CD-Recording Problems..........178
Rectifying Music-Playback Problems 186

Glossary 190

Index 193

How to Use This Book

As you read the chapters in this book, you'll find lots of pictures, figures, and diagrams to help you visualize what you're reading. You'll also find numerous pictures, or icons, that serve as cues to flag important information or provide directions. Here is a guide to help you understand the pictures you'll encounter in this book:

 A Note identifies a relatively important piece of information that will make things easier or faster for you to accomplish on your PC. Most notes are worth reading, if only for the time and effort they can save you.

 A Warning gives notice that an action on your PC can have serious consequences and could lead to loss of work, delays, or other problems. Our goal is not to scare you, but to steer you clear of potential sources of trouble.

 The CD-ROM flags additional materials including exercises and animations that you will find on the CD-ROM included with this book. Because some materials work better on your PC than in print, we've included many activities and exercises. These help you become more familiar with your system while practicing important skills.

 Because PC information and online resources are so dynamic, some material related to this book, including Web-based training, resides on the **www.LearnwithGateway.com** Web site. This allows us to keep that information fresh and up to date.

 The *Survive & Thrive* series includes several books on topics from digital photography to the Internet. Where other titles can be useful in improving and expanding your learning, we use the Book icon to draw those titles to your attention.

 Gateway offers a hands-on training course on many of the topics covered in this book. Additional fees may apply. Call 888-852-4821 for enrollment information. If applicable, please have your customer ID and order number ready when you call.

You'll find sidebar information sprinkled throughout the chapters, as follows:

> ### More About . . .
> The More About . . . information is supplementary, and is provided so you can learn more about making technology work for you. Feel free to skip this material during your first pass through the book, but please return to it later.

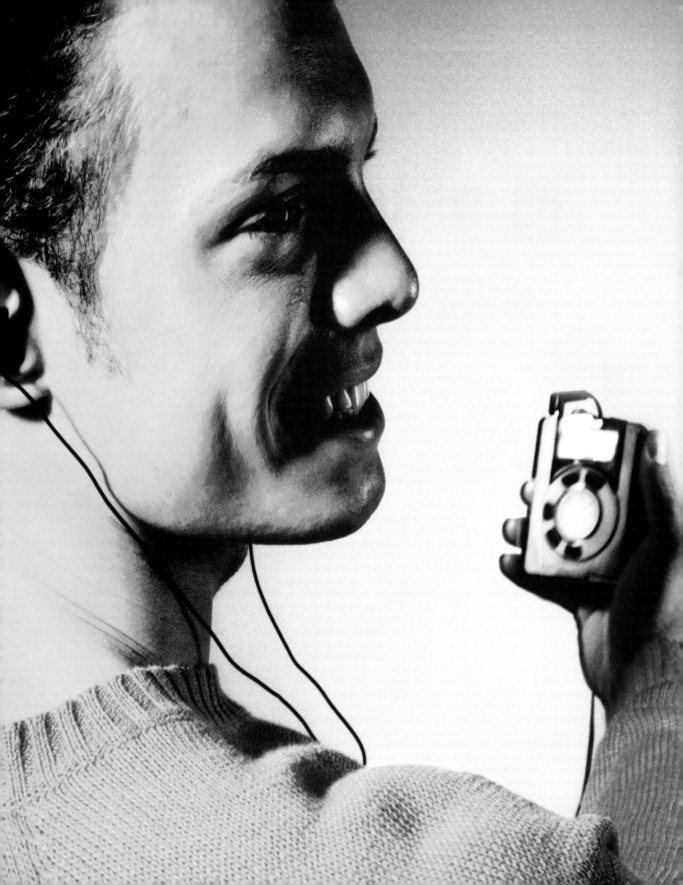

CHAPTER 1

The Road to Digital Music

2   Making the Journey from Analog to Digital
Learn how music is recorded

8   Reaping the Benefits of Digital Audio
Quality, compression, and real-time streaming

More than a hundred years ago, when Thomas Edison recorded the strains of "Mary Had a Little Lamb" using his patented phonograph, a cultural revolution began. In days past, music, though culturally important, was as fleeting as mist; if you weren't present to witness a live performance, it was lost to you. With the advent of the sound-recording revolution, however, we waltzed to the phonograph in our parlors, we huddled around our radios for the latest news and shows, and we slapped 45s on our turntables to hear the latest single from the nation's newest stars. Our ability to hear the same radio programs and record albums regardless of whether we lived in Portland, Maine or Portland, Oregon strengthened our cultural identity, and created a giant sound-recording industry to boot.

These days, a new revolution is underway: digital recording. Although this revolution may not have the profound cultural impact that Edison's sound recording inspired, it does vastly improve the quality of sound recordings, and more significantly, enables common consumers to use their computers to download, store, copy, and listen to music. That means that among other things, you can create your own custom compilation CDs from songs you've stored on your computer's hard disk. You can even copy songs from your computer to a portable audio player, and listen to your favorite music on the go!

 Of course, no good revolution is without controversy, and the digital music revolution is no exception. You'll learn about the controversy surrounding digital music in Chapter 3.

In this chapter, you'll find out just how the sound-recording industry got started, and why it transitioned from using analog technology to record sound to using digital technology. Finally, you'll discover the benefits of using digital technology.

Making the Journey from Analog to Digital Recording

Ever since Thomas Edison's first crude sound recordings in 1877, musicians and engineers have strived to accurately reproduce sound. First, sound engineers relied on analog technology to record sound, storing sound information on tin-foil cylinders and, later, vinyl records and magnetic tape. These media, though considered adequate in their time, were hampered by imperfections. However, a shift to digital technology in the 1980s revolutionized sound recording, heralding vast improvements in the field. In fact, today's recordings are almost indistinguishable from live performances.

Understanding the journey from the scratchy tin-foil recordings of years past to the near-perfect recordings on compact disc today is helpful to understanding how digital recording works and what benefits digital audio brings. For this reason, we've outlined a brief history of analog and digital recording here, explaining how each technology works, and discussing the strengths and weaknesses of both.

Analog Recording

Every sound you hear—be it music, words, or bumps in the night—travels to your ears in *analog* format. That is, the sounds are created in continuous waves, without any breaks. In fact, if you analyze a typical sound of any type using an *oscilloscope* (a tool used to measure sound and electronic waves), you can see the unbroken sound wave, like the one in Figure 1-1. The fluctuations in the wave correspond to the high and low tones in the sound, called gradations.

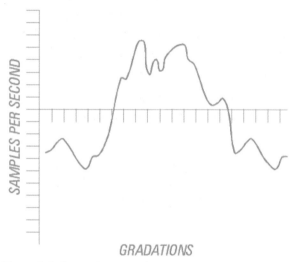

Figure 1-1 An analog sound.

A Brief History of Analog Recording

Not surprisingly, early attempts to record sound involved the use of analog techniques in the hopes of mirroring the original sound as accurately as possible. For example, Thomas Edison's phonograph, invented in 1877, used a horn, a sharp needle, and a rotating tin-foil cylinder to record sound. The horn collected the sound, whose waves caused the needle to vibrate up and down according to the pitch and volume of the sound, which in turn scratched grooves into the surface of the rotating foil cylinder.

To play back a recorded sound, this process was simply reversed. The listener placed another needle (though not as sharp) on the foil cylinder to listen from the phonograph. As the cylinder rotated, the needle rode through the grooves in the foil, reproducing the sounds that had been cut into the cylinder. The phonograph's horn amplified vibrations from the needle, making them audible to the listener.

Although the use of tinfoil cylinders to record sound gave way to vinyl records, the essentials of Edison's sound-recording techniques remained the same: a vibrating needle was used to cut patterns into a rotating medium. With vinyl, however, a master disk could be created, which could then be used to stamp out millions of replicas—which you (or your parents) could buy at a local record shop. These records were played back on phonographs equipped with their own needles; special circuitry translated the needle's

vibrations into electronic signals that could be amplified and broadcast through one or more speakers or headphones.

For decades, vinyl records remained the key medium for analog sound recordings, despite patents for other analog sound-recording technologies. Foremost among these recording alternatives was the tape recorder, developed by German doctor Fritz Pfleumer in 1931. This technology used a microphone to convert sound waves into magnetic signals, which were then encoded on analog tape. This magnetic field on the tape could be "read" by a playback head, which generated electric energy that could be boosted in an amplifier and converted into sound by a speaker. This technology became significantly more popular when the Philips Company released a cassette tape geared toward consumers in the early 1960s, enabling members of the general public to make their own sound recordings cheaply and easily.

Drawbacks to Analog Recording

Despite the popularity of analog recording over the years, this technology has its limitations. No matter how thin the needle, how dense the magnetic field, or how involved the recording process, an analog recording can't reproduce the sound generated by a live event with absolute precision. The sound wave associated with such performances is complex, with a large range of loud and soft sounds. This prevents even the best analog-recording equipment from creating an exact reproduction of the sound wave.

Another drawback of analog recording is that it introduces extraneous noise and distortion (referred to as *background noise*) into the recording process, especially when copies of a recording are made. If you've ever used a photocopier to make a copy of a copy of a document, you're already familiar with this fact; the more removed you are from the original, the lower the quality of the copy. Likewise, each time you copy a copy of an analog recording, the less the copied recording sounds like the original.

Compounding these issues, playing back an analog recording creates a few obstacles of its own—namely, the hisses and pops that occur when a record player's needle passes over a record's groove or when a tape deck's head reads the magnetic tape.

Digital Recording

Fortunately, analog recording is no longer the only game in town. Relatively new on the scene is digital recording, a technology that emerged in the early 1980s with the release of audio CDs (compact discs). With digital recording, a sound wave, no matter how complex, is converted into a sequence of zeroes and ones (or on and off), known as bits (short for binary digits). This sequence of bits is stored in a data file, the same type of file used by personal computers.

When you play back a digital recording, a computer within the playback device assigns each number in the sequence an electronic signal; these signals are played in order, to reproduce the original sound.

How closely the digitally recorded sound matches the original one depends on a couple factors:

✦ **Sampling rate.** This refers to the number of times per second a sound wave is measured, or *sampled.*

✦ **Quantization.** This refers to the number of bits a sample contains.

Sampling Rate

Sampling is the process of converting sound to digital bits. A *sample* is a binary number that represents the amplitude of the sound being recorded at a given moment of time. Figure 1-2 illustrates sampling in action; each bar in the figure is a sample, or digital "snapshot," which captures a specific section of the original sound's pitch and volume.

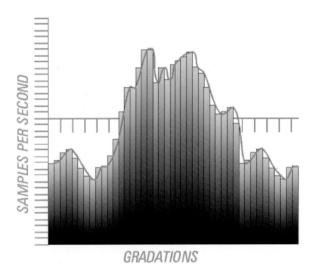

Figure 1-2 Digital sampling.

As mentioned previously, the quality of a digital recording depends in part on the sampling rate. That is, how many samples are taken per second. The more samples a recording takes per second, the more accurate the recording of the original sound. That's because each sample captures a shorter segment of the original sound, and as a result, doesn't have to average any changes in pitch or volume. This is illustrated in Figure 1-2, in which the bars (samples) are close enough together that the shape they form is very close to the shape of the original wave. If there were fewer bars in the figure, the sound quality would not be as clear; if there were more bars, the sound would be improved.

> **More About . . . Sampling Rates**
>
> So just how often should a sound be sampled? A hundred times per second? A thousand? Incredibly, most audio CDs are recorded at a sampling rate of 44,100 samples per second. (Anything less, and the human ear can detect the difference in quality.) DATs (Digital Audio Tapes), on the other hand, use an even higher sampling rate, making them popular for high-end recording.

Quantization

Although it's impossible to overstate the importance of sampling rate with respect to the quality of a digital sound recording, another important factor is *quantization*. This refers to the size of each digital sample in a recording, measured in bits. When it comes to sample size, the smaller the sample, the more accurate the musical recording. So, for the best quality recordings, you want more samples (a higher sampling rate) and smaller samples (a smaller sample size).

How small should each sample be? Commercial CDs typically contain samples that are 16 bits in size, representing 65,536 different levels of sound. This guarantees a high-quality sample, which, assuming the sampling rate is adequate, ensures a high-quality overall recording.

Reaping the Benefits of Digital Audio

As mentioned earlier, analog recording has a few drawbacks—namely, an inability to adequately capture complex sound waves, a propensity for background noise, and the pops and hisses associated with the playback of an analog recording. With digital recording, however, these problems are solved. For example, listen to the same song on vinyl and then on CD; the difference in quality is often staggering. In addition to improvements in quality, digital recording offers increased versatility over its analog counterpart. For example, recorded digital sound can be stored on numerous media, including the hard drive in your computer.

Quality

When recorded at a high sampling rate and with a high level of quantization, digital recordings mirror the original sound far more accurately than analog recordings do. This is because most analog recordings are plagued by a low *signal-to-noise ratio* due to high background noise. That is, the *signal,* or the part of the recording you want to hear, is weak compared to the background noise. Digital recordings have a very high signal-to-noise ratio, meaning the signal is strong, with background noise virtually nonexistent.

The advantages of digital recording are only further revealed when copies of the recording are made. Unlike analog recordings, a copied digital recording maintains consistent sound quality no matter how far removed it is from the original. That's because instead of storing sound information in grooves on a record or on magnetic tape, it's stored in an electronic file that can be copied bit for bit, just as a word-processing document can be copied from your hard drive to a floppy disk with no loss of letters, words, or sentences. Whether a digital recording is the master copy, or is a copy a thousand times removed, quality can remain the same. As a result, the CD you buy in a store has the exact same quality as the original digital studio recording.

Versatility

As mentioned previously, a digital recording exists as a series of bits in a data file—the same type of file used by computers. This storage method makes digital recordings very versatile. Like other computer files, such as word-processing documents, files containing digital recordings can be copied, edited, and deleted. They can also be stored on CDs, DVDs, computer hard drives, and so on. Likewise, just as other computer files can be downloaded over the Internet or sent from your computer to other electronic devices, so too can files containing digital recordings. Figure 1-3 shows some music files stored on a computer.

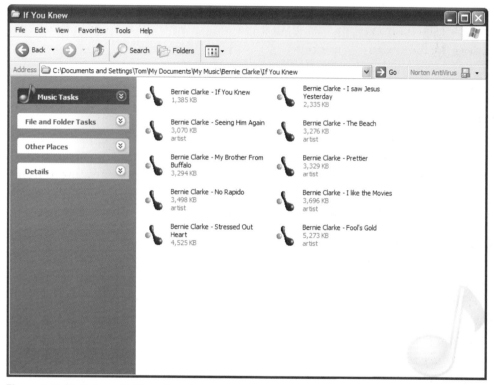

Figure 1-3 Digital music files stored on a computer.

Unlike most other computer files, however, files containing digital recordings typically contain extraordinarily large amounts of data. For example, a CD-quality audio file of a three-minute song typically consumes nearly 32 MB (megabytes) of disk space! To put that into context, a single megabyte can hold one million typed characters, equivalent to about two issues of the average magazine. A single song, then, is equivalent to 64 issues.

Compact discs can store roughly 650 MB of data, plenty of room for an album's worth of song files. Those files, however, are simply too large to be downloaded over the

Internet in a timely manner. Likewise, storing multiple 32 MB music files on your hard drive would leave little space for anything else. To resolve this problem, the computer industry developed a way to make digital audio files smaller, while retaining much of their original quality. This process is called *data compression.*

Data Compression

The data-compression process uses a piece of software called a digital audio encoder to determine what sounds in a digital audio file can be heard by the human ear. Then, it removes any sounds outside that range. As a result, digital audio files become significantly smaller, enabling easier download over the Internet and storage on a computer hard drive. For example, MP3, a popular digital audio format (discussed in detail in Chapter 5), reduces the size of digital audio files by a 12 to 1 ratio. That 32 MB song now consumes less than 3 MB of disk space—and is small enough that it can be quickly downloaded from the Internet via a normal dial-up connection!

For your convenience, Table 1-1 compares the download time for a 32 MB and a 3 MB file.

Table 1-1 Downloading a 32 MB and a 3 MB file.

DOWNLOAD SPEED	32 MB FILE	3 MB FILE
28.8 Kbps dial-up	2 hours 46 minutes 40 seconds	15 minutes 37 seconds
56 Kbps dial-up	1 hour 14 minutes 24 seconds	6 minutes 59 seconds
640 Kbps DSL/cable	6 minutes 40 seconds	37 seconds
1.5 Mbps T1	2 minutes 46 seconds	15 seconds

Another way to make digital audio files smaller is to use a digital audio encoder to lower the sampling rate, thereby lowering the amount of recording data stored in the file in the first place. Of course, reducing the sampling rate also reduces the sound quality; fortunately, most digital audio encoders let you choose from several different sampling rates so you can strike the right balance of file size and sound quality. Most listeners don't mind slightly reduced sound quality to produce smaller files. At lower sampling rates, digital audio sounds a lot like FM radio; at higher sampling rates, the sound can be near-CD quality.

Streaming

In addition to compressing files and lowering their sampling rates to make it easier to download audio over the Internet, another technology is used: streaming audio. With *streaming audio* (also called *Webcasting*), you can listen to the first part of an audio file while the rest of the file is still downloading. If immediate gratification is important to you, you'll especially appreciate this technology. It's also ideal for broadcasting live concerts, news reports, and sporting events. Listeners can listen to events unfolding in real time, even though the audio file isn't yet complete.

To enjoy this technology, simply use your Web browser to tune into a streaming audio site (see Chapter 6), and listen—in real-time—to all sorts of digital recordings and events.

To Keep on Learning . . .

Go to the CD-ROM and select the segment:

✦ *Digital Music Overview* to learn more about digital versus analog music and the advantages of digital music.

Go online to **www.LearnwithGateway.com** and log on to select:

✦ *Internet Links and Resources*

✦ *FAQs*

With the *Survive & Thrive* series, refer to *Use and Care for Your PC* for more information on:

✦ *Copying, editing, and deleting files*

Gateway offers a hands-on training course that covers many of the topics in this chapter. Additional fees may apply. Call **888-852-4821** for enrollment information. If applicable, please have your customer ID and order number ready when you call.

CHAPTER 2

Enjoying the Digital Music Revolution

16   Recording Digital Music

Convert your favorite songs to digital audio files

18   Appreciating Digital Music's Versatility and Portability

Listen to music anywhere, anytime

23   Finding New Music and Sharing

Locate music on the Web and share your tracks

If you explore the annals of history, you'll realize that nearly every revolution—be it a war or a cultural movement—has been about freedom. For example, during the American Revolution, the American colonists, in response to the English crown's measures of taxation and control, fought to overthrow that repressive government thus, through independence, gain their freedom. Likewise, the Industrial Revolution succeeded in freeing many workers from the overwhelming poverty that pervaded life in the 17th century.

The digital music revolution is no different; admittedly, the stakes aren't quite so high. This revolution won't unshackle the downtrodden worker or free struggling colonists from burdensome taxation. It will, however, enable those who love music in all its forms to enjoy the freedom of recording their own music compilations using nothing more than their trusty home computer. In addition, they can listen to that music whenever and wherever they like using any number of electronic devices, discover music they might not have found otherwise, and share music with others in ways never before thought possible. This chapter explores the many ways in which digital music liberates listeners to enjoy their music any way they please.

Recording Digital Music

In the old days, recording your favorite song involved pressing your 8-track tape recorder against one of your hi-fi's speakers while the song played on the radio or on your turntable. In addition to capturing the sweet sounds of your stereo, the tape recorder typically also picked up all background noise, including the less melodious tones of your mother, yelling at you to turn the music down.

Eventually, tape decks enabled you to use cassette tapes to record the music on your stereo independently of the speakers, which made for better-quality sound. This recording method, however, was time consuming. Recording an entire album's songs meant staying put until the album was finished. In addition, because an entire album wouldn't fit on one side of a cassette, you had to turn the cassette, and the album, over halfway through the recording and make sure the cassette didn't cut off the last song.

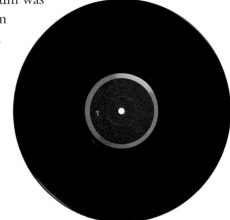

Even more time-consuming was the process of making your own compilation tape filled with your favorite songs from a plethora of artists. By the time you sifted through all your (unalphabetized) albums, sorted them in the order you wanted them, placed each one on the record player in turn, pressed all the appropriate buttons on your tape deck to record, and stayed put through each song to make sure none of them ran over, you could easily wile away hours of your free time.

Thanks to the digital music revolution, however, times have changed. These days, you can quickly and easily record high-quality copies of your favorite songs using nothing more than your home computer and a few minutes of your time.

Most people who make digital music recordings do so by converting existing music from an audio CD to digital audio files (such as MP3 files or some other format), a process called *ripping*. Ripping digital recordings from audio CDs is a quick process. Depending on the software you use and your system's configuration, you can rip a song from a CD in as little as one-fourth the time it would take to listen to the song. In fact, you can convert an entire CD to digital audio computer files in a matter of minutes.

> ### More About . . . Recording Music
> You can even convert all your classic vinyl or cassettes that are stashed away in the attic to digital audio files on your computer—an option made only more intriguing by the fact that you can then use computer software to easily clean up imperfections in your analog recordings. (You'll learn how to record your own CDs, and convert albums and cassettes to digital files in Chapter 7.) As an added benefit, these digital files will almost certainly last longer than your aging albums and tapes—not to mention being easier to carry around!

Thanks to digital music, however, you're no longer limited to simply recording the songs you like. Using software installed on your computer, you can edit the songs you record, moving the pieces around and putting them back together however you see fit. You can even use pieces of songs from completely separate recordings to create entirely new songs, a process known as *sampling*.

In addition, your ability to record digital music isn't limited to material that has already been produced. You can use this technology to record your own music or sounds through a microphone, or connect a keyboard or guitar to your computer and play your music directly into the computer. If you have a digital music idea, chances are you can achieve it and have fun in the process.

Appreciating Digital Music's Versatility and Portability

As mentioned in Chapter 1, digital music offers improved sound quality and versatility over its analog counterpart because the quality doesn't degrade no matter how many copies are made of a music file. Although this is a major component of the success of digital music, it's the versatility of this medium that has really instigated the digital music revolution. Thanks to digital recording, music can be stored on CDs, DVDs, MP3 disks, computer hard drives, and more—and played back using any number of devices, including computer players, portable players, car-stereo players, and home-stereo players.

Using Your Computer to Listen to Digital Music

To pump digital music through your computer speakers, you simply use a digital music player program that you install on your computer. Figure 2-1 shows the interface for Windows Media Player. After the player is installed, you can listen to music files stored on your hard drive or on other media. These players are easy to use, and in most cases can perform the following functions:

2

✦ Play commercial audio CDs from your CD drive

✦ Play digital music files

✦ Pause, stop, rewind, and fast-forward playback via push-button controls

✦ Create and store lists of songs—called *playlists*—to play in order or randomly

✦ Download from the Internet song, album, and artist information about the currently playing song

 There are many players to choose from; you'll learn about several in Chapter 5.

Figure 2-1 The Windows Media Player interface.

In addition, you can use your computer to listen to digital music or other recordings played on countless Internet radio stations. To do so, however, you must have a *streaming audio player* installed on your computer; this is a type of computer program that enables you to listen to a sound file even before it's finished downloading to your machine or, in the case of Internet radio, to listen to a sound file that is essentially continuous (that is, has no beginning or end). There are several types of streaming-audio players.

 You'll learn more about using your computer to listen to Internet radio in Chapter 6.

Listening to Digital Music on the Go

Because digital music is so versatile, it's also incredibly portable. You can listen to digital music anywhere, any time, with little or no change in quality or service—a phenomenon commonly referred to as *universal access*. Thanks to this universal access, you can enjoy your favorite digital music whether you're sitting in front of your computer, baking cookies in your kitchen, driving your car, roller-skating on the boardwalk, fishing the Atlantic, or meandering through your local park.

Digital music's portability may strike a deep chord in you if you remember the days when the only way to enjoy music on the go was to heft a giant stereo, often called a "boom box," onto one shoulder. In those days, only the highly coordinated could enjoy listening to their own music while engaged in an athletic endeavor such as roller-skating or, for that matter, walking.

Of course, the release of the Sony Walkman signified a giant step in portable music. Instead of hoisting your player onto your shoulder, you could slip it into your pocket. Unfortunately, even with a Walkman, music fans were limited in how much music they could listen to on the go. After all, a single cassette tape could hold, at most, only 90 minutes of music. If you planned on being out for a while, it meant you'd have to listen to the same tape over and over, or you'd have to carry multiple tapes—no small feat for someone on roller-skates.

Then enters digital music. Although early portable digital music players, such as the portable Rio® player introduced by Diamond in 1998, contained enough memory to store about 20 minutes of CD quality music, advances in digital music technology have yielded portable players that enable you to store literally thousands of songs in a compressed digital format, possibly your entire CD collection. Incredibly, these devices are no larger than a portable CD player, enabling you to carry them with you everywhere you go. Another benefit of portable digital music players is that the music doesn't skip if the unit is jarred, because there are no moving parts associated with playing the music.

 You'll learn more about portable digital music players in Chapter 4.

However, today's portable digital music players provide more options than just added capacity. For example, many enable you to play music files in a variety of formats. Others include FM radio tuners, for those times when you want to listen to live radio.

Digital music players aren't just for roller-skaters. For example, many car-stereo manufacturers have been swept up in the digital music revolution. Only a few years ago, digital music players in cars were almost non-existent; these days, however, every major car-stereo manufacturer either has or is planning to release a digital audio-capable unit.

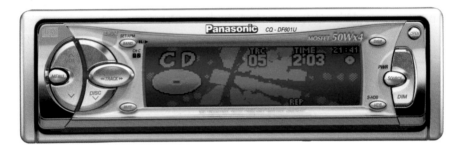

Many models incorporate MP3 CD playback, enabling you to travel with one MP3 CD containing a hundred or more of your favorite songs instead of lugging around dozens of CDs on a road trip.

 The biggest hurdle car-stereo manufacturers faced in this arena wasn't integrating digital music technology into an automobile; it was getting the music files into the car. Stereo manufacturers developed several different solutions, from removable players that connect directly to a computer, to units that use removable memory cards, to CD players that read digital audio files in addition to standard audio CDs.

Not to be outdone, many companies that manufacture home-stereo systems have jumped on the digital music bandwagon. For example, some digital home-audio products play the files you've already created and stored on your computer through your home stereo system. Others take things one step further and operate completely independent from your computer, recording music directly from CDs onto internal storage components.

 See Chapter 4 for more on audio and home stereo digital music components.

And the best is yet to come. As technology advances, digital music is more and more prevalent. Launched in 2001, XM Radio uses satellites and digital transmission to provide continuous music anywhere in the world. Imagine, no more music-less drives through the Sonoran desert: you and a friend can listen to the same song at the same time from the same broadcast even if you're on opposite sides of the country.

There are also products on the horizon that will allow you to pause, rewind, and save live radio for later, much like Digital Video Recorders (such as TiVo) do for television broadcasts today. For example, imagine you caught the tail end of a traffic report. With these new products, you'd be able to rewind the live radio to hear the report that you missed. No longer bound by the need to physically connect to a computer, digital music is even making the leap from your desktop to your mobile phone and PDA (personal digital assistant). Wireless communication is advancing as fast as digital music, and the combination of the two is exciting. Very soon, you'll be able to store all your digital music files at home and play them from anywhere in the world, even without another computer. And, with the right set up, you can let your friends play them as well.

Finding New Music and Sharing

In addition to ripping music from your collection of CDs, you can also obtain digital audio files by downloading them from the Internet. In fact, the Web features literally hundreds of Web sites offering digital audio file downloads, each with its own selection of music.

Some of these sites, including various digital audio archives, offer music free of charge; as a result, however, they don't always have a vast selection of songs from big-name artists. These sites do, however, offer a great way for upcoming artists to gather a following of fans.

You might want to visit any of several sites that don't store their own files, and instead function as search engines for music stored on other sites. These sites enable you to search many other sites at once for music in the format(s) you specify. See Chapter 6 for more on these sites.

Other sites, such as the ones run by record companies or by other officially licensed companies, charge users a monthly fee. These Web sites, called *subscription music services*, enable users to download a set number of songs each month. These subscription sites are, in general, very easy to use, but typically offer only those songs released by a particular record label. That means you'll need to subscribe to multiple services if you want to be able to download songs from multiple labels.

Some record companies and other legal distributors allow you to purchase electronic copies of single songs instead of paying a monthly fee. In fact, this is how some record labels distribute releases by new artists who might not generate enough response to support retail audio CD production costs. This distribution method saves shipping costs, and can be secured to ensure that only the designated recipient uses the file.

Still other sites enable you to share music files with other Internet users. Not surprisingly, however, the practice of sharing files with others opens some sticky legal issues. The copyright laws involved are very intricate, and at present, the United States judicial system is reviewing the entire practice. You can be sure, however, that as digital music technology advances, the technology to prevent copyright infringement will also advance.

 You'll learn more about the legal issues surrounding digital music in Chapter 3; for information about sharing files, see Chapter 6.

TO KEEP ON LEARNING . . .

 Go online to www.LearnwithGateway.com and log on to select:

 ✦ *Internet Links and Resources*
 ✦ *FAQs*

 Gateway offers a hands-on training course that covers many of the topics in this chapter. Additional fees may apply. Call 888-852-4821 for enrollment information. If applicable, please have your customer ID and order number ready when you call.

2

CHAPTER 3

Security and Legal Issues

28 Explaining Copyright Law
Learn why copyright law exists

30 Understanding Copyright Holder Rights
Find out what's protected by copyright

32 Knowing Your Consumer Rights Under Copyright Law
Examine consumer rights

34 Finding U.S. Copyright Laws
Keep up-to-date with the copyright debate

There has been much discussion recently regarding digital music and possible copyright violation. The potential for copyright violation has led to a new situation between the recording industry and the users of digital music. For example, if you watch the news regularly, you might be familiar with the name Napster. Napster and the RIAA (Recording Industry Association of America) have been in and out of the courts over the last few years regarding copyrights held by the music industry and the distribution of digital music over the Internet. In this chapter, you'll learn what this means to you and how to make an informed decision about copyright in regards to digital music.

Explaining Copyright Law

Before you can understand how copyrights affect digital music, it's important you understand what a copyright is. A *copyright* is a set of laws designed to make sure that the person who creates something (a piece of art, a computer program, a Web site, a movie, a piece of music, etc. . . .) is protected from other people claiming it as their own. Copyright laws also protect the people who pay for the creation of material, like record companies or movie studios. Copyright holders and copyright owners are virtually the same (either the creator or the person who paid for the creation) and the terms are used interchangeably in the law. Part of the copyright allows the owner (holder) to do whatever he or she likes with the copyrighted material, including selling copies of the material to others.

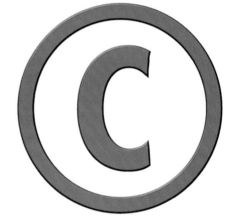

The idea of copyrights has been around for a long time. Greek scholars in the ancient world wanted to be sure they were given due credit for their work. Then, when the printing press was invented in 1450, authors wanted to be assured they were recognized as the creator of a work. However, the first law instituted to protect authors from piracy wasn't passed until 1709. It was called the Statute of Anne and was passed by the British Parliament. In addition to recognizing the author as the owner of a copyright, the Statute of Anne established a term for the length of the copyright. These principles are still seen in today's copyright laws.

In 1886, the Berne (in English, it's pronounced "burn") Convention started as a declaration for protecting creative works and stands as the basis for International and United States copyright laws. In essence, the convention is made up of a number of countries that agree to protect art, literature, music, and other things such as intellectual property.

In October of 1988, the U.S. Congress passed the Berne Convention Implementation Act. This amended U.S. copyright laws to comply with the Berne Convention for the Protection of Literary and Artistic Work. Two of the key copyright issues in this law are:

✦ You have a copyright on everything you create, whether you ever publish it or not, as long as you're a citizen of a county recognizing the Berne Convention.

✦ The Berne Convention recently extended the length of individual copyrights from 50 to 70 years after the life of the original copyright holder. U.S. copyright laws use the same terms.

Although the idea of copyright has been around for hundreds of years, it's not without controversy—here in the United States and around the world. Before 1998, copyrights held by corporations were valid for only 75 years. This means if this law were still in effect, some of the original Mickey Mouse artwork would no longer be protected under copyright law, but would be considered part of the public domain. In 1998, Congress passed the Sonny Bono Term Extension Act that extended the copyright by twenty years. Also in 1998, Congress passed the DMCA (Digital Millennium Copyright Act), which implemented two WIPO (World Intellectual Property Organization) treaties passed in 1996: the WIPO Copyright Treaty and the WIPO Performances and Phonograms Treaty. The DMCA also addresses potential copyright infringement protection for computer users and online service providers. Parts of the WIPO treaties (and consequently the DMCA) deal with technological protection of copyrights. These laws attempt to provide greater protection for the copyright holder while still allowing fair use of the copyrighted material to the public.

However, in February 2002, a group of publishers and individuals petitioned the Supreme Court to review the 1998 Sonny Bono Term Extension Act's constitutionality. Whether the Supreme Court's ruling will have any effect on digital music remains to be seen, but it's an indication of how important copyright law issues have become.

To understand the key legal issues in accessing and using digital music, go to the CD-ROM segment *Digital Music and Copyright Law.*

Copyright law protects every book, magazine article, software program, movie, record, and other publicly distributed material. You can see copyright information by looking on the back of the case of an audio CD you purchased, as shown in Figure 3-1. If the work is copyrighted, you'll see the copyright symbol (©), the copyright holder, and the year of the copyright. In books and magazines, the copyright information is generally on the inside cover. You can even check the inside cover of this book to see who holds the copyright on this material.

Figure 3-1 Typical copyright information provided for a music CD.

 Copyright law doesn't require a copyright holder to display the copyright symbol or list all the copyright information. If the copyright holder lists the information, it's easier to bring legal action, if necessary. If they don't display the information, however, it doesn't mean the material is considered public domain.

Understanding Copyright Holder Rights

The copyright holder can do whatever he or she likes with the copyrighted material. This includes making multiple copies of the material, selling copies of the material, grouping copyrighted material together into a compilation, and then distributing the compilation.

 To find more detailed information on copyright holder rights, see the table at the end of this chapter.

Copyright laws also protect the copyright holders from people making money from the material without paying the copyright holder. For instance, a record distributor contracts to sell music on behalf of the copyright holder with the understanding that the distributor will pay the copyright holder a fee for each copy of the music sold. If a distributor does not pay the fee (called a royalty), the distributor is violating copyright law.

Copyright law provides different benefits for copyrights held by corporations than those held by individuals. Copyrights held by corporations are valid for 95 years under the current laws. Copyrights held by the creator of the material are valid for the life of the individual, plus an additional 50 years. After the copyright expires, the material transfers to the public domain and others can use it without paying royalties to the copyright holder.

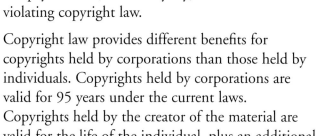

More About . . . Copyrights and Corporations

In many cases, people don't own copyrights, corporations do. The details of who owns the copyright are generally spelled out when the contract is written. The companies that distribute and sell the material hold the copyrights for many books, movies, and music. You'll learn more about this later, but it's important to know there's a distinction in the law.

When it comes to music, the record companies hold most of the copyrights. They are most likely not held by the individual performers. If the performers also wrote the songs, they may have the copyright for the lyrics, but the record company may have the copyright for the recording performance that eventually is sold to the public on a CD or tape. It can get very confusing.

To give you an example of how many copyrights can be involved, look at your favorite music CD. The back of the CD contains the copyright information for the CD itself (generally held by the record company). Now, open the CD case and look at the enclosed booklet, if there is one. Each of the songs listed has information on who wrote the song and the corresponding copyright. In fact, the booklet itself may be copyrighted! It can be quite a task to keep up with all the different copyrights.

Because of the current copyright laws, new original recordings are copyrighted and the information on who owns the copyright is easy to find. But consider a new recording by the London Symphony Orchestra of one of Beethoven's Symphonies. The original music wouldn't be covered under today's copyright laws. However, the recording is protected under the copyright held by the record company and, perhaps, the Symphony itself. If the recording happened to be video taped by the BBC (British Broadcasting Corporation) for broadcast, the BBC owns the copyright for the video. So three or four companies or individuals could hold copyrights on a single performance.

Knowing Your Consumer Rights Under Copyright Law

When it comes right down to it, how does copyright law affect you and your venture into digital music?

 To find more detailed information on consumer rights, see the table at the end of this chapter.

When you purchase a CD, you can use it for personal use, within reason. You can make a copy of the CD as long as you don't give that copy to someone else or sell it for profit. You can also make digital music files from the songs on the CD without violating the copyright; you just can't give them to anyone else. In fact, specific laws protect your right to copy music for personal use. The Audio Home Recording Act says, in part, that no action can be brought against you for copyright infringement, if you make a copy of the material for "private, noncommercial use."

So why wasn't casual copying of copyrighted material much of an issue before now? Teenagers have made compilations of songs, often called "mix tapes," for their high school friends for years without any interference from the record companies. However,

the record companies haven't always looked the other way. When personal tape recorders were introduced, the recording industry was afraid that people copying records onto tape would impact their business. As a compromise, they agreed that the price of every blank audio cassette would include a small fee paid to the record industry to compensate for the potential use of their material. When recordable CDs were introduced, this fee was applied to their sale as well.

But CDs and digital recording introduced an unexpected technical difference over previous recording techniques. Because of the mechanics involved, when copying videotapes with a VCR, the copies are a lower quality than the original. But computer CD players and recorders make perfect copies of songs on CDs. You could easily make a copy of a copy of a copy and the quality of the recording would be the same as the original.

 In a somewhat controversial move, some record companies are introducing CDs with copy protection built-in. This copy protection makes it difficult, if not impossible, to make copies of the music. However, many users find this copy protection also prevents them from even playing some CDs in their CD players. It's being reviewed as to whether this violates consumer rights under the Audio Home Recording Act.

The copyright holder has the right to distribute the material and determine who can distribute it. Your rights as a music consumer, even with the Audio Home Recording Act, don't include distributing someone else's copyrighted work.

If you use your computer to create unique digital music, copyright law protects your creation just like it protects the music on a CD you bought in a store. Even if you never publish your music, the copyright law in the Berne Convention Implementation Act protects you.

 To find more detailed information on the Berne Convention Implementation Act, see the table at the end of this chapter.

If you choose to register your copyright with the Library of Congress, there's a registration fee. But no matter what, if you own the copyright and eventually sign that

big record deal, you can rest assured that you're protected.

Finding U.S. Copyright Laws

In the U.S., the Library of Congress manages copyrights. You can find everything you ever want to know about U.S. copyrights through the Library of Congress. As the governing body over U.S. copyright, the Library of Congress is responsible for making sure that all copyrighted material is handled correctly. The Library of Congress Web site, shown in Figure 3-2, contains vast amounts of information on copyright law and copyright infringement. The Web site updates current legislation and court action in the news section. If you have additional questions about U.S. copyrights and how they apply to digital music, check out the Library of Congress Web site.

 For information on how to get to the Library of Congress Web site, see the table at the end of this chapter.

Figure 3-2 The Library of Congress Copyright Office Web site.

The United States participates in a number of worldwide organizations that attempt to ensure that copyrights are protected internationally. Through U.S. participation in these organizations, and through direct copyright agreements with other countries, copyrights granted in the U.S. are protected in nearly 100 countries. Along the same lines, copyrights granted in other countries are also often protected here. Unfortunately, the U.S. does not have copyright agreements with all countries. This situation has allowed music and software piracy to run rampant in some countries.

At the moment, U.S. copyright laws have the most impact on digital music creation, use, and distribution. This is partially because of the Internet's prevalence in the United States, but it's also because the American record companies are engaged in the distribution of digital music files.

 Copyright is a complex and rapidly evolving area of the law and you should contact a legal expert before making any unauthorized copies of music in any format. Opinions or comments expressed here should not be taken as legal advice.

3

To Keep on Learning . . .

 Go to the CD-ROM and select the segment:

✦ *Digital Music and Copyright Law* to understand the key legal issues in accessing and using digital music.

 Go online to **www.LearnwithGateway.com** and log on to select:

✦ *Internet Links and Resources*
  ✦ *Copyright*
  ✦ *Music News*
  ✦ *Digital Music Copyright*
  ✦ *Music Licensing*
  ✦ *Industry Associations*
✦ *FAQs*

 Gateway offers a hands-on training course that covers many of the topics in this chapter. Additional fees may apply. Call **888-852-4821** for enrollment information. If applicable, please have your customer ID and order number ready when you call.

CHAPTER 4

Audio Hardware Components

40   **Exploring Audio Hardware**

   Discover the computer devices for superior audio capabilities

53   **Tuning Into External Audio Devices**

   Enjoy your digital music away from your computer

Now that you know just how revolutionary digital audio is, you probably can't wait to listen to some digital music—not to mention record your own. However, to enjoy listening to digital music's enhanced capabilities using your computer, you'll need some specific computer hardware. Fortunately, if you just bought a new computer (or have had one for a while), chances are it came equipped to play sounds, music, and other types of audio right out of the box.

There's a broad range of sound hardware you may want to add to your computer to expand its capabilities and enhance your audio enjoyment. In addition, you may choose to purchase hardware devices—such as portable digital music players, home-stereo digital audio players, and car-stereo players—that enable you to listen to your digital music as you exercise, drive, cook, etc. In this chapter, you'll look at the audio hardware available for listening to and creating digital music both on your computer and while you're on the go.

Before you hurry to your local electronics store or favorite Web site to buy new sound equipment, try recording, editing, and playing some music using what came with your computer. You might find the quality is sufficient. But if it's not, read this chapter to find out how you can enhance your audio experiences.

Exploring Audio Hardware

Most computers are equipped with a sound card (explained later) and a set of speakers. These two hardware devices are the minimum requirements for playing music through your computer. The sound card and speakers that come with most computers are adequate for most audio needs. True audiophiles, however, may find the audio produced by their computer's original sound card and speakers to be bland and without depth in comparison to the audio produced by their home or car stereo.

Not sure whether your computer is equipped with a sound card and speakers? If you purchased it within the last few years, there's a good chance you have both. To find out for sure, simply listen to your machine as you work. If you hear sounds when Windows starts or when you receive an e-mail message, you know your system is equipped for sound.

Just as you need the right tools to improve your car's performance, you need the right equipment to boost the quality of your computer's sound—namely, a sufficiently powerful computer, a quality sound card, a good set of speakers, and a good CD/DVD drive.

 To gain insights on being able to choose the right hardware components for your digital music system, go to the **CD-ROM** segment *Right Hardware: Choosing.*

Computer System Requirements

Your computer is equipped with hardware, including a CPU (Central Processing Unit), RAM (Random Access Memory), and hard-drive space. These are some of the core operating elements of a computer. For optimal digital audio performance, a computer running Microsoft® Windows® XP should meet the Microsoft recommended requirements. Here are the recommendations:

✦ 300 MHz CPU or better

✦ 128 MB RAM or more

✦ At least 5–10 GB of hard-drive space

If you want to use your computer to play music in the background while you work in one or more other open programs, you might need a computer with an even faster processor and more RAM. Likewise, when you get more into your music, you may want to store large numbers of music files on your computer. In which case, you'll probably need more hard-drive space—perhaps as much as 100 GB. Of course, you can always start smaller and install an additional hard drive on your computer if you run out of space on the original.

Defining a Sound Card

A *sound card* is a hardware component that converts data in an audio file to sound, which is then played through your computer's speakers. Additionally, if you're recording audio using a microphone, the sound card captures the audio and sends it to the computer software you use to record. As mentioned earlier, if you can hear sound on your computer, your system has a sound card.

Sound cards are sometimes integrated into (built on) a computer's motherboard, but can be a separate *expansion card* that plugs into the motherboard (like a video card or a modem). If your audio needs are simple, involving the playback and occasional recording of CDs, an integrated sound card will most likely meet your needs.

Integrated sound card

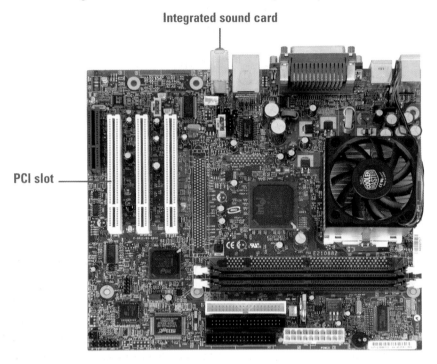

PCI slot

If, however, you plan to edit digital music, listen to surround-sound movies, or play high-end immersion-environment games (games whose sounds seem to come at you from all directions), an expansion card is the sound card for you. If you add an expansion card sound card to a computer that already has a built-in sound card on the motherboard, the on-board sound card is automatically disabled in favor of the expansion sound card.

To determine whether your system's sound card is integrated or an expansion card, check your paperwork for your computer or call the company from which you purchased the computer. You can also determine this by opening your computer's system unit case. If the sound card is plugged into a *PCI* (Peripheral Component Interconnect) or *ISA* (Industry Standard Architecture) slot, you have an expansion card sound card. If not, you have an integrated sound card.

 In addition to internal sound cards, discussed here, external sound cards are also available. You'll learn about external sound cards later in this section.

Choosing the Right Expansion Card

If you decide you want to buy an expansion card or just want to evaluate the sound card you already own, here are the essential features:

✦ **PCI.** *PCI* refers to the slot type used by the sound card to connect to the motherboard. PCI offers the best connection for internal sound cards.

✦ **3D Audio support.** This refers to a sound card's ability to support true surround sound with four or five speakers and a sub-woofer—a must if you value a true surround-sound experience with your computer. There are two versions of 3D Audio: EAX (the format created and supported by the sound cards produced by Creative Labs, such as the SoundBlaster® Live!™) and A3D (the format supported by most other sound-card vendors). Most games and audio software capable of producing surround-sound audio can use either type of 3D Audio format.

✦ **SoundBlaster® compatibility.** Because the SoundBlaster card was among the earliest and most popular on the market, many audio programs were designed to work with it. For this reason, nearly all sound cards today use SoundBlaster audio commands to ensure they will work with most audio software.

✦ **DirectAudio capability.** *DirectAudio* is the audio component of the DirectX® architecture from Microsoft. *DirectX* is the core Windows technology that drives high-speed multimedia and games on the computer.

✦ **Wave table synthesis.** Sound cards produce sound using one of two methods: FM synthesis or wave table synthesis. *FM synthesis* mimics the sound produced by various sound-producing devices from a table of pre-defined formulas, which usually results in audio that's slightly off. *Wave table synthesis*, on the other hand, reproduces audio from recordings of real instruments, producing much more realistic sound. However, sound cards that use wave table synthesis are a bit more expensive than their FM synthesis counterparts.

◆ **High decibel signal to noise ratio (dB SN Ratio).** All electronic means of creating sound produce unwanted noise. This ratio measures how well a card produces quality sound that is louder than the electronic baseline noise created by your computer. The higher the rating, the better the sound; a sound card rated at 92 dB SN Ratio is a good bet.

◆ **Full duplex.** A sound card with full-duplex capabilities can play and record audio at the same time, and also enables you to hold normal conversations using Internet telephone or video conferencing. Fortunately, most new sound cards are full duplex.

◆ **At least three input/output connections.** Most sound-card connection ports are ⅛-inch stereo jacks, like the ones found for headphones on portable radios. These are usually labeled speaker (or output), line in, and line out. You can use the *speaker/output* connection to connect a speaker set or headphones, the *line in* connection to connect another audio source such as a tape player, and the *line out* connection to play your computer's audio output using your home stereo or other another audio component. Any additional connections can be used for a microphone, MIDI input, or other specialized connections.

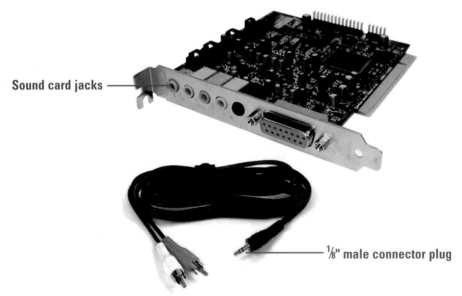

Sound card jacks ——

—— ⅛" male connector plug

 Consult your favorite games' and audio software's manuals to see which manufacturers' sound cards are listed as fully compatible or supported. If you're not sure, ask a salesperson at your computer store for a recommendation.

Opting for an External Sound Card

If you're looking for a sound card that adds high-end audio-processing capabilities to any computer, including notebooks, you might want to consider an external sound card. These cards are often connected to the computer via a USB or IEEE 1394 FireWire®. FireWire is a trademark of Apple® computer and is a part of the IEEE 1394 standard. Some external sound cards are completely external components (similar to the way printers or scanners are external components), whereas others may be installed into a full-sized drive bay (similar to the way a CD drive is installed internally). Creative Labs seems to be the front-runner in this new type of computer audio component with its Extigy and Audigy products.

 Most people don't need high-end audio-processing capabilities, but if you really want a realistic audio experience on your system or you just want your music to sound the best it can, you may want to consider getting an external sound card.

In addition to offering the best sound processing available to computers, external sound cards offer a serious advantage over internal sound cards—namely, connections. These devices boast a wide range of connection types to simplify the hassles of connecting your computer to portable audio devices or even your home stereo.

Selecting Speakers

We've looked at sound cards. Now it's time to investigate computer speakers. When choosing a set of speakers for your computer or evaluating your existing set, here are the essential issues:

✦ **Whether to get a two-speaker set or a multi-speaker set.** Two-speaker sets include a left and a right speaker, typically placed in front of you, to produce stereo sound. A multi-speaker set, on the other hand, includes a front left, front right, rear left, and rear right speaker to produce sound from all directions. In addition, a multi-speaker set may include a front-center speaker and a sub-woofer. The sub-woofer can be placed anywhere in the room because low-frequency sounds are *omni-directional* (you can hear them from any direction). The more speakers in your speaker set, the more realistic the sound immersion will be. *Sound immersion* refers to the experience of hearing sounds, as they would actually occur—that is, from all directions. The more realistic the sound immersion, the more it seems you're attending the concert, auto race, or flight battle whose sounds your speakers are broadcasting.

 Another selection issue is traditional versus slim line speakers. Traditional speakers are usually thicker from front to back to accommodate the cone-shaped speaker components. Slim line speakers are usually thinner from front to back because they use a flat panel to produce sounds. Traditional speakers usually focus sound in a single direction like a spot light. Slim line speakers usually produce optimal sound in all directions like a bare light bulb.

✦ **What kind of speaker sets your sound card supports.** If your sound card does not support multi-speaker surround sound, you need a two-speaker set. If your sound card supports high-end audio capabilities such as surround sound and multiple speakers, you should select a speaker set that matches those specifications. For example, a two-speaker set cannot accurately reproduce Dolby Digital sound.

If you're getting poor sound, you may need to change your speakers or your sound card. To determine which is the most likely culprit in producing bad sound, connect your speakers to another audio source, such as a home stereo CD player. If the audio is still poor, upgrading your speakers is required. If the audio is good when you connect to your home stereo, maybe your computer's sound card needs upgrading.

If, however, you're a serious audiophile and want excellent speakers to match your computer's audio capabilities and your discerning ear, you may want to upgrade from the ones that came with your system. In that case, look for a speaker set with the following features:

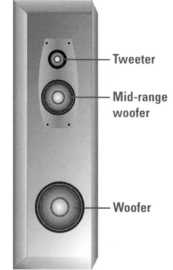

✦ **Two-way, three-way, or better speakers.**
Most individual speakers are in fact comprised of two or more speakers within its cabinet or case. An individual speaker with three speakers in its case is called a three-way system. A *three-way system* uses a woofer for low-range frequencies and a tweeter for high-range frequencies, plus a *mid-range woofer* for middle frequencies. The more speakers there are in an individual speaker's case, the smaller the range of frequency handled by each one. That means more power can be applied to each range, resulting in better sound at a higher volume.

Tweeter

Mid-range
woofer

Woofer

✦ **High decibel signal to noise ratio (dB SN Ratio).** As with sound cards, the decibel signal to noise ratio (dB SN Ratio) is important with regard to speakers; as before, the higher the rating, the better the sound.

✦ **A broad frequency response range.** A speaker's frequency response range indicates the frequency range the speakers can reproduce. As you approach the extremes of this range, the quality of the sound decreases. Very good speaker sets have a frequency response range of 35 Hz to 20 kHz.

✦ **A large power rating.** Speaker power is rated in watts, which measures how much power each speaker can receive and still adequately reproduce sound. In most cases, the higher the power rating, the better the quality of sound the speaker can produce. Good speakers have a rating of at least 20 watts. Excellent speakers have a rating of 100 watts or more.

 Some speaker sets are rated in total watts, where the ratings of each speaker are added together. Other speaker sets rate each speaker individually. The ratings noted in the preceding bullet refer to individual speakers.

Selecting a CD/DVD Drive

CD-ROM (compact disc-read only memory) drives have been standard equipment on most computers for nearly a decade, making it easy to install programs, view data, and play audio CDs. CD-ROM drives, however, are lacking in one area. Although they can read data from discs, they cannot write data to discs. In digital-audio terms, this means you can use a CD-ROM to listen to music, but not to burn your own CDs. If you only have a CD-ROM drive in your computer, this section will help you choose a recordable disc drive. If, however, you just want to upgrade your existing recordable disc drive, this section will help you choose a new and improved model.

 The process of creating your own CDs (and DVDs) is called *burning*. When you burn a CD, you copy files from your hard drive or another source onto the CD. In the case of audio CDs, once a CD is burned, you can listen to it just as you would a CD you bought at your local music store. Although you can also burn audio files to DVDs, this is not yet a common practice.

Choosing a Recordable Disc Drive

To burn your own CDs, you need a recordable disc drive. These days, many new computers include recordable disc drives. If the drive installed on your computer doesn't quite meet your needs, you may want to upgrade or add a new one. There are a couple types of CD-recordable drives you should be aware of:

◆ **CD-R.** A CD-R (compact disc-recordable) drive can read data from CD-ROM discs, play audio CDs, and write to CD-R discs. These types of drives aren't that common anymore. (Note that a *CD-R* disc is a writable CD that can be written to only one time. Once burned, a CD-R becomes a CD-ROM.)

◆ **CD-RW.** A CD-RW (compact disc-rewritable) drive has the same capabilities as a CD-R drive, but can also be used to record data to the same CD multiple times, even erasing the CD and reusing it. (For this to work, a special type of CD must be used, called a *CD-RW.*)

 You can buy either internal or external recordable disc drives. External drives are useful if you don't have any room left inside your computer or they can also be used with laptops.

 To gain information about storing music on recordable CDs, go to the CD-ROM segment *CDs and Recordable CDs.*

Just as you can use a CD-recordable drive to burn CDs, you can also burn your own DVDs using special DVD-recordable drives. As mentioned previously, DVDs are typically used to store items such as full-length movies, but they can also be used for digital music. Many DVD drives also enable you to burn CDs, making them a good choice if you want to be able to record several different types of information using your recordable drive.

When it comes to DVD-recordable drives, you have a few options:

◆ **DVD-R.** Similar to a CD-R drive, a DVD-R (digital versatile disc-recordable) drive can read data from DVD-ROM discs and write data to DVD-R discs. Like CD-R discs, a DVD-R disc is a writable DVD that can be written to only one time. Once burned, a DVD-R becomes a DVD-ROM. Like CDs, DVDs enable you to store audio files. Unlike CD recorders and discs, however, DVD recorders and discs use much narrower tracks, allowing them to store up to seven times more data than CDs. That's why you commonly find full-length movies stored on DVDs.

◆ **DVD+RW.** DVD+RW (digital versatile disc+rewritable) is another leading standard for recording data to DVDs. DVD+RW drives function like standard CD-RW drives, enabling you to record data to the same disc multiple times. DVD+RWs are limited to 1,000 rewrites and can store 3.95 GB of data per media side. DVD+RWs are used primarily to create master DVDs for mass duplication.

◆ **DVD-RAM.** DVD-RAM (digital versatile disc-random access memory) is a leading standard for recording data to DVDs. A DVD-RAM drive can read information on DVDs and write information to DVD-RAMs, which can be written to multiple times. DVD-RAMs can be rewritten over 100,000 times and can store 2.6 GB of data per media side. DVD-RAMs are more flexible than DVD-RWs in how data is written to them and are therefore more widely used on home computers.

Table 4-1 summarizes the uses for each type of CD and DVD drive.

Table 4-1 Types of CD/DVD drives and uses.

TASK	CD-ROM	CD-R	CD-RW	DVD	DVD-R	DVD+RW	DVD-RAM
Play CDs	Yes	Yes	Yes	Yes	Yes	Yes	Yes
Read data CDs	Yes	Yes	Yes	Yes	Yes	Yes	Yes
Burn CD-Rs	No	Yes	Yes	No	No	No	No
Burn CD-RWs	No	No	Yes	No	No	No	No
Play DVDs	No	No	No	Yes	Yes	Yes	Yes
Read data DVDs	No	No	No	Yes	Yes	Yes	Yes
Burn DVD-Rs	No	No	No	No	Yes	Yes	Yes
Burn DVD-RWs	No	No	No	No	No	Yes	No
Burn DVD-RAMs	No	No	No	No	No	No	Yes
Many recordable drives are, in fact, combination players, performing more than one function. For example, some CD-RW drives can also play DVDs, and most DVD drives can also record CDs. Note, however, that you may need to purchase two drives to record every possible type of media.							

Understanding Drive Speed

Once you've decided what type of drive you want—that is, whether you want a CD-RW drive, a DVD-R drive, a combination drive, or what have you—you'll need to decide how fast you want that drive to be. The faster the drive, the faster the reading and/or writing operations will occur. The read and write speed of a CD/DVD drive is measured in relation to an audio CD's playback rate. For example, a 52x CD-ROM drive reads CD media 52 times faster than an audio CD normally plays.

Drives have a speed rating for each of their functions. That means, for example, that a CD-RW drive that is capable of burning CD-Rs, burning CD-RWs, and reading CDs/CD-Rs/CD-RWs has three speed ratings. These ratings are always listed in the order of CD-R burning, then CD-RW burning, and then CD reading. For example, the Yamaha CRW3200EZ CD-RW drive has a speed rating of 24x10x40—or 24x CD-R burn speed, 10x CD-RW burn speed, and 40x CD read speed.

DVD burners are a new technology and like the first CD burners, most only operate at 1x normal DVD playback speed. Some 2x burners have been produced. As this technology matures, expect faster DVD burners to become available. Because the CD-RW format uses a different (and slower) method to record information onto the CD media, CD-RW burn speeds are typically half that of CD-R burn speeds.

Drive speed is particularly important when it comes to burning CDs and DVDs. Burning an entire CD can take more than 60 minutes at 1x speed, 30 minutes at 2x speed, 15 minutes at 4x speed, 8 minutes at 8x speed, and 4 minutes at 16x speed. If you plan to record CDs on a regular basis, you'll appreciate a drive that supports faster speeds!

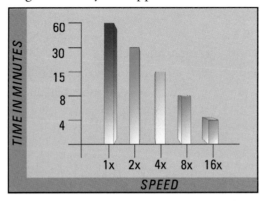

 When burning a CD or DVD, you must make sure that the media's burn speed rating meets or exceeds that of the burner. Otherwise, the burner will attempt to write to the media faster than it can handle, resulting in a failed burn (a.k.a. creating a coaster). The burner attempts to burn at its fastest rate by default. If you only have media with a speed rating lower than that of your burner drive, configure your burning software to use a slower burn rate to prevent failed burns.

More About . . . Mass-Producing CDs

Suppose you're the lead singer of a band, and you've just recorded your first album. To cut costs, you're considering mass-producing the CDs yourself using your CD burner. Unfortunately, however, no matter how fast your CD burner is, you'll only be able to burn CDs one at a time. That means if your band hits it big, you'll be too busy slaving over your computer to burn copies of your hit CD to enjoy the fruits of your success.

If you're really interested in mass-producing CDs, you'll need more than a single computer to do it. With additional computers, each with fast recordable drives, your ability to mass-produce your disc is multiplied. Alternatively, you can purchase a dedicated CD duplicator device, which can simultaneously burn as many as 10 CDs from a master CD. These devices, however, are very expensive. A third,  and perhaps more practical, option is to contract with a media-duplication company. These companies can duplicate just about any type of computer or audio media. To locate one, check your local Yellow Pages under "media duplication" or "audio services."

Tuning Into External Audio Devices

When it comes to the tools you can use to listen to digital audio, sound cards, speakers, and CD/DVD drives are only the tip of the iceberg. In fact, with the right cables and connection ports, you can connect your computer to just about any external audio source or playback device, be it your home stereo or a portable player. You can even use your computer to enable your car stereo to play your music files. In this section, you'll learn about the different external audio devices you can use to enjoy digital music.

Connecting Your Computer to Your Home Stereo

Connecting your computer to your home stereo is as easy as plugging in a mouse. One of the benefits of connecting your computer to your home stereo is that doing so enables you to play audio files stored on your computer through your home stereo's speakers. However, there's one problem you must overcome: *connection-type mismatch.* That is, the audio connections on most computer sound cards are ⅛-inch stereo jacks, whereas most home-stereo equipment uses either RCA jacks or optical connections.

If you have an external sound card, you may have RCA jacks, digital jacks, or even optical jacks at your disposal. In that case, you need only get a link cable long enough to make the connection. If, however, your sound card has only ⅛-inch stereo jacks, you need a converter to match the connections on your home stereo. Converters can be found online or at most electronic stores.

We suggest you get a connection cable with a ⅛-inch male stereo jack on one end and two male RCA jack connectors at the other—one for left speaker sounds, typically colored white, and one for right speaker sounds, typically colored red. (RCA connectors colored yellow are usually for video.) Use a high-quality cable to make the computer-to-home stereo connection. Be sure to note which set of RCA ports you use, because that will determine what setting you tune the receiver to in order to hear the computer audio. In addition, you can also record audio from your home stereo to your computer. To do so, connect the RCA out connectors on the home stereo to the line in jack on your computer's sound card.

To be able to connect your computer to a stereo system, go to the CD-ROM segment *PC to Stereo: Connecting.*

Digital Music Players for the Home

If your computer is in your home office or some other private part of your house, chances are it's far, far away from your home stereo—making the possibility of connecting the two systems somewhat remote. This geographic distance, however, should not dissuade you from enjoying your computer's digital music files on your stereo. These days, you can purchase full-sized computer audio playback stereo components, which connect to your home stereo in the same way as a CD player or tape deck might. Once your player is hooked up, you can use it to play audio files from its hard drive, from a data CD, or from a memory card (also called a memory stick). Simply copy the files you want to play from your computer to any of these portable storage media, insert the media into the digital music player, and let the tunes begin.

 Digital music players for your home stereo are typically a bit more expensive than other more common components, such as CD or DVD players. As this type of device becomes more popular and widespread, however, the cost is sure to come down.

Portable Players

The ability to listen to music on the go is not new. What is new, however, is the ability to store thousands of minutes of music—enough for your entire CD collection—in a device that fits in your shirt pocket, and to use that device to listen to any of those files you please, anywhere, anytime. How? Using a portable digital music player.

Put simply, portable digital music players are audio devices that play music stored in digital form on internal memory cards or on miniature hard drives. These portable players support the use of several digital file formats. In addition, most portable players feature the following:

 You'll learn more about file formats in Chapter 5.

✦ A readout screen that shows the name of the artist and song currently playing, as well as other information such as playback time remaining

✦ Playback control buttons built right into the device or a remote control smaller than a credit card

✦ Intuitive software that allows you to create digital music files from your own CDs, download files from the Internet, and exchange content between the player and your computer

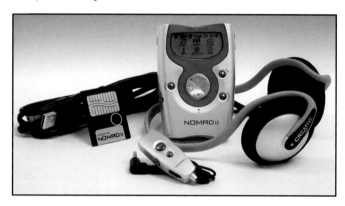

To transfer content from your computer to your digital audio player, you typically connect the two machines using USB or FireWire (1394) ports. Once a portable digital music player is connected to your computer, it usually appears as a removable storage device similar to a floppy or a CD-RW. To load music into a portable digital music player, simply copy music files to the new storage-device icon in My Computer or Windows Explorer. When you're ready to listen to your music through the player, simply disconnect it, attach the headphones, and use the player's playback controls to play your music.

 To be able to copy music to a portable device, go to the Web segment *Music: Copying to Portable Devices* within the Windows Media Player lesson.

There are two types of portable digital music players:

✦ **Players with memory cards.** These players typically can store anywhere from 32 to 256 MB of audio files on a removable memory card.

Memory card players have no moving parts so sudden movements and vibrations will not interrupt playback.

✦ **Players with a hard drive.** These players feature hard drives ranging in size from 10 to 30 GB, meaning you can copy significantly more music onto it than you can a memory card player. For example, a 30 GB hard drive can hold more than 500 hours of music, the equivalent of nearly 1,000 CDs.

You must prevent hard drive-based models from being jarred or dropped. Sudden movements and vibrations can not only interrupt playback, but can also damage the hard drive.

Dual-Mode Digital Audio/Audio CD Players

If you're a real audiophile, you probably already have an enormous CD collection—so big, in fact, it would take you a lifetime to convert every disc to an audio file format, no matter how fast the CD drive on your computer was. A music player that combined the features of a portable CD player with a computer's ability to play audio files would be right up your alley!

Fortunately, just such a device exists. Known as a *dual-mode CD player*, these players play both regular CDs, as well as CD media containing digital audio files. Unlike traditional CDs, which can hold only about 80 minutes of music, CD media containing audio files can store more then 10 hours of music. Of course, your computer must have CD-burning capabilities for you to truly enjoy using this type of player.

The only drawback to this type of player is that it's as prone to shock-induced skipping as any portable CD player. That means you probably can't use it while jogging or playing other sports. If, however, you can keep the player a bit more stable, such as by placing it on the seat of your car or on your desk at work, you can get the benefit of extended audio playback via audio files.

Dual-mode CD players are usually comparably priced to quality CD-audio only playback devices, and can be found in both portable and home stereo-sized models. In addition, some DVD players enable you to play back audio files from CDs burned using a computer.

Digital Audio Players for Your Car

If you've ever been on a road trip, you know what a pain it is to lug enough CDs around to see you to your destination. These days, however, several car-stereo manufacturers sell digital audio players that operate in much the same way as portable digital music players. Many models incorporate digital audio file CD playback, enabling you to travel with one CD containing a hundred or more of your favorite songs instead of lugging around dozens of CDs. Others can play back songs stored in a hard drive or memory card.

 Digital audio players that use hard drives or memory cards employ removable versions of storage devices or the entire player is removable for easy connection to a computer for audio file transfer.

Digital audio players for cars are typically fairly expensive, especially when compared to typical car stereos or even portable digital audio playback devices. Chances are, however, that prices will fall as these devices become more popular and widespread.

4

Other Playback Devices

Audio capabilities have found their way into numerous other devices not initially designed as music playback tools. For example, some phones, personal digital assistants, pagers, and pocket-sized computers enable you to play back many audio file types. (In most cases, you'll need headphones or external speakers to hear audio playback.) However, because these devices are typically not geared toward using multimedia, their storage capacities are limited because of their use of memory cards instead of hard drives.

 If the capability to play back audio files is not built into a device, you can often obtain expansion cartridges or docking modules to add audio capabilities. The cost of these add-on units vary greatly.

Go to the CD-ROM and select the segment:

✦ *CDs and Recordable CDs* to gain more information about storing music on recordable CDs.

✦ *Right Hardware: Choosing* to gain insights on being able to choose the right hardware components for your digital music system.

✦ *PC to Stereo: Connecting* to be able to connect your computer to a stereo system.

 Go online to **www.LearnwithGateway.com** and log on to select:

✦ *Windows Media Player*

✦ *Internet Links and Resources*

✦ *FAQs*

 With the *Survive & Thrive* series, refer to *Use and Care for Your PC* for more information on:

✦ *Basic use of a CD/DVD drive*

✦ *How CD burners work*

 Gateway offers a hands-on training course that covers many of the topics in this chapter. Additional fees may apply. Call **888-852-4821** for enrollment information. If applicable, please have your customer ID and order number ready when you call.

CHAPTER 5

Audio Software Components

62   Understanding Digital Audio Formats

Pick the right file format for playback and recording

67   Choosing a Digital Music Player

Find and download the best software for your needs

77   Using Your Digital Music Player

Listen to your favorite songs, on your computer

J ust as you needed a record player to play LPs, a tape deck to play cassette tapes, and a CD player to play your compact discs, you need a digital music player to play audio files on your computer. The difference? Unlike record players, tape decks, and CD players, all of which are hardware components, a computer digital music player is a piece of software installed on a computer. (In fact, odds are that one of them came preinstalled on your computer.) You play digital music by using your mouse to click the buttons that appear in the digital music player program's window.

Thanks to digital music's newfound popularity, recent years have seen an explosion of digital music players on the market. Although you can use all these players to listen to audio files, important differences do exist between players. In this chapter, you'll learn about the most popular digital music formats and player programs. You'll also learn to choose the right player for your personal needs.

Understanding Digital Audio Formats

Before you get into the nuts and bolts of choosing a digital music player, it's a good idea to gain some understanding of the various digital audio file formats commonly used today. That's because certain digital music players support only certain types of files. By knowing the advantages and disadvantages of each file format, you can better decide which digital music player will best meet your needs.

The phrase *file format* refers to the way in which information in a file is encoded; different programs are designed to handle files of different formats. Take word-processing programs as an example. Microsoft Notepad can handle files that use the TXT (text) format and Microsoft Word can manage files that use the DOC (document) format. Some word-processing programs can handle different types of word-processing files; for example, you can use Microsoft WordPad to open and edit a DOC file. Other word-processing programs, however, cannot.

— Microsoft Word document

— Image file

— Microsoft Excel spreadsheet

— Text document

— Windows Media Player file

Likewise, different digital music players work with different types of files, supporting some file formats but not others. These file formats vary in sound quality and file size, each with its own strengths and weaknesses. For example, WAV, a commonly used uncompressed file format, boasts good quality, but a large file size. If your music files use this file format, they'll quickly consume any available space on your hard drive. Fortunately, other formats offer smaller file sizes.

 As you learned in Chapter 1, music files are often made smaller through a process called *data compression*. When a music file is compressed, a digital audio encoder is used to determine what sounds in the file are audible to the human ear, and removes any sounds outside that range. This means that although the quality of the file is technically degraded, you may not be able to tell by listening to it.

The two most popular compressed file formats for recording your own digital music files are MP3 (Moving Pictures Expert Group Audio Layer 3) and WMA (Windows Media Audio). Most digital music players work with both formats. MP3 and WMA, however, aren't the only formats in town. As shown in Table 5-1, there are many different digital-music file formats.

 To find more technical information on digital music file formats, see the table at the end of this chapter.

Table 5-1 Common digital audio formats.

EXTENSION	FORMAT
MP3	Widely adopted format that uses data compression to produce high-quality audio in relatively small files. MP3 files are often used to make hard-disk copies of music from CDs.
WMA	MP3 alternative with similar audio quality at a smaller file size.
AAC	New file format from Dolby Labs that produces high-quality sound at low sampling rates.
CDA	High-quality file format used on commercial audio CDs.
LQT	MP3 competitor from Liquid Audio®, with increased security features.
MID or MIDI	Used to reproduce instrumental music in very compact files, often for background music on Web pages and in online games.
MPC	The supposed successor to MP3, capable of producing higher-quality files; the official name is MPEGplus.
RA	Developed by Real Networks, this RealAudio format was originally designed for real-time streaming-audio feeds.
RM	The Real Network format designed for streaming movie (or "media") files; can also be used to stream digital audio files.
VQF	An older digital audio format, inferior to the MP3 format, and no longer officially supported.
WAV	A widely used file format (pronounced "wave"). This is the standard format for Windows system sounds, and is also used on many Web pages.

No matter what type of file, you can determine its format by looking at the three-letter *file extension* appended to the end of the file's name. For example, files whose names end in ".mp3" are MP3 files. Likewise, files whose names end in ".wma" are WMA files.

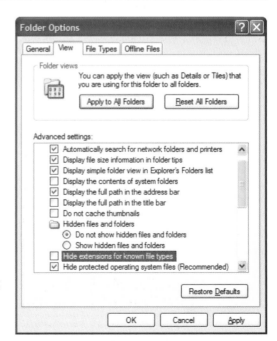

If you're using Windows XP in the default view, you won't see file extensions. However, the computer has to have them to know what program to use to access the file. To view the file extensions in the My Music folder, open the folder. Select **Tools**, and then choose **Folder Options**. In the Folder Options dialog box, select the **View** tab, and uncheck the **Hide extensions for known file types** box.

Click **Apply** and then click the **Close** button (the X in the upper-right corner). When you open My Music, you'll notice that your filenames now display the file extensions.

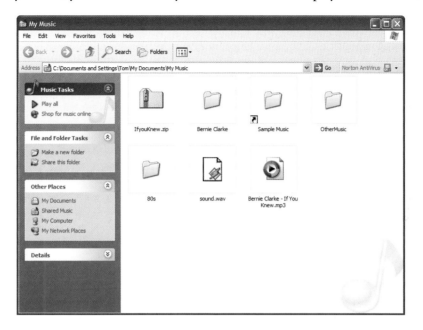

 Windows XP hides the file extensions from users by default because the icons already show the associated program and to protect users from removing this association. If you feel more comfortable not viewing the file extensions, please reverse the preceding instructions to go back to the default view.

Several of the most common of these formats are discussed in the following list:

MP3. The MP3 digital audio file format compresses music while still maintaining near-CD quality sound. In fact, MP3's data compression reduces digital sound files by about a 12:1 ratio. This combination of features—small file size (and thus quickly downloadable) plus high-quality sound—has made MP3 the most popular digital music file format. Indeed, it's no exaggeration to say that MP3 has taken the music industry by storm.

 Because of its obvious benefits, MP3 is the file format you'll encounter most. There is, however, a newer format: MPEGplus. Commonly referred to as the MPC format, MPEGplus encodes CD-quality sound in smaller-sized files than other comparable formats. In the future, MPEGplus may replace the MP3 format.

WMA. The WMA format, designed by Microsoft, offers sound quality similar to MP3, but with even smaller file sizes. As with MP3 files, you can control the sampling rate used when recording WMA files. (Remember, the higher the sampling rate, the higher the sound quality—and the larger the file size.)

Unlike MP3, however, the WMA format uses *copy protection*, a feature that works by creating an official *license* for each song you copy. Copy-protected audio files play back only on the system that recorded them; when you copy a file to your computer, your computer—and *only* your computer—is authorized to play the song. By using Windows Media Player to copy that song from your computer to a CD or portable device, however, you can copy the song's license, enabling you to listen to the song using multiple devices.

 Most digital music players automatically enable WMA copy protection, by default. In most cases, you can turn off copy protection for new files you record by accessing the player's recording options. See "Making Your Own Digital Audio Files" later in this chapter to learn how to access recording options in Windows Media Player.

AAC. Dolby Labs developed the AAC (Advanced Audio Coding) digital audio format, which creates music files at low sampling rates that sound better than higher-rate files encoded with MP3 and other formats. It's not in widespread use yet, but is one of several next-generation formats that could eventually replace MP3 as the digital audio format of choice.

CDA. The CDA (compact disc audio) format is the standard file format used on commercial audio CDs. Unlike most other file formats, such as MP3 and WMA, CDA is uncompressed, which results in high-quality sound, but also very large files. For this reason, it's not commonly an option for storing digital music files on your computer's hard disk. If, however, you want to play your home-recorded CDs in your home or car stereo, they will need to be in this format.

LQT. LQT (Liquid track) isn't widely used for consumer recording, but you will find some commercial music downloads in this format. That's because LQT's built-in security features make copying files more difficult than with other formats. For example, you can't convert LQT files to MP3 or WAV formats, which means you can't burn LQT files to CD. For this reason, many large record companies favor Liquid Audio's LQT format for putting their music online.

MIDI. Although MIDI (Musical Instrument Digital Interface) is a music file format, it doesn't record actual music. Instead, it records information about music. For example, a MIDI file might contain information that describes a melody played by a violin—the note values and pitches—without recording the actual performance. It's kind of like how a player piano works. The MIDI player plays back the notes as "recorded" in the original performance. This format is also widely used by Web developers for background music on Web sites. Because it doesn't record any actual instruments or voices, however, it's not (and cannot be) used to digitally copy music from CDs and other sources.

MIDI does not support the recording of voice; it's strictly used for instrumental recording.

RA. Real Networks' RA (RealAudio) format is the format of choice for streaming audio over the Internet. As you learned in Chapter 2, and will explore further in Chapter 6, you can use *streaming audio* to listen to audio files before and while the entire file is downloaded. Broadcasters often use the RealAudio format to transmit audio for live concerts, sports, and other events as they happen.

 Although the RealAudio format is an effective format for streaming audio, you probably won't use it to create your own digital music files.

WAV. If your computer runs Windows, you're already familiar with the WAV (waveform audio) file type—even if you don't realize it. That's because the sound you hear automatically each time Windows starts is a built-in WAV file. WAV files store uncompressed sound-wave data, making them larger than their MP3 or WMA counterparts. Because WAV file are uncompressed, their audio quality is very good but, as you probably guessed, their file size is quite large. For this reason, you'll rarely find digital music files in the WAV format on the Internet.

 When you burn audio files to a CD, these files will usually be converted to the WAV format. The WAV files are then converted to CDA format so that the CD you record can be played in other CD players (besides your computer).

5

Choosing a Digital Music Player

Most digital music players share a similar basic feature set, which means that no matter which one you choose, you'll be able to enjoy a core set of tools. For example, most digital music players enable you to do the following:

+ Play commercial audio CDs.

+ Play digital music files in several popular formats, including MP3, WMA, WAV, and so on.

+ Pause, stop, rewind, and fast-forward playback via push-button controls, similar to those found on your home CD player. Most digital music players also include Next and Previous Track (song) buttons, along with a volume control and mute button.

✦ Store lists of songs, called *playlists*. A playlist can contain the individual tracks of a CD or individual files on your hard drive. In addition, you can create your own playlists to better organize the music you like to listen to most or to set up a group of songs for burning onto a CD.

✦ Play songs in the playlist's predefined order or randomly.

✦ Use the Internet to download song, album, and artist information about the track that is currently playing. Some players even use the Internet to provide access to detailed artist biographies, or to enable you to purchase the CD online.

✦ Display CD artwork or colorful visual displays to accompany the music.

✦ Resize the player on your desktop to consume more or less space.

✦ Change the look and feel of the player's controls and interface by applying a new skin.

 You'll learn more about skins—what they are and how to apply them—later in this chapter.

In addition, to enable you to play your music, create playlists, and the like, many digital music players also include full-blown encoding and CD-creation capabilities. These players are often referred to as *all-in-one programs*. In the next sections, you'll learn about several of the more popular digital music players.

 Also referred to as *ripping* or *copying, encoding* is the process of copying a digital audio file to your hard drive from a music CD or from the Internet.

Comparing Players

If you run Microsoft Windows® 98 or later, you already have a digital music player installed on your computer: Windows Media Player (occasionally abbreviated as WMP). If not, you can easily download Windows Media Player or any other digital music player from the Internet. When you do, you usually have three choices:

 You'll learn how to download digital music players later in this chapter in the section "Downloading a Music Player."

✦ **Download a freeware program.** Freeware programs are programs you can download and use at no charge. Most digital music players available on the Internet are freeware programs.

✦ **Download a shareware program.** Shareware programs are programs that you can try for free, but must purchase after a designated evaluation period to continue using them.

✦ **Download a commercial program.** Commercial programs are programs you must pay for to use.

5

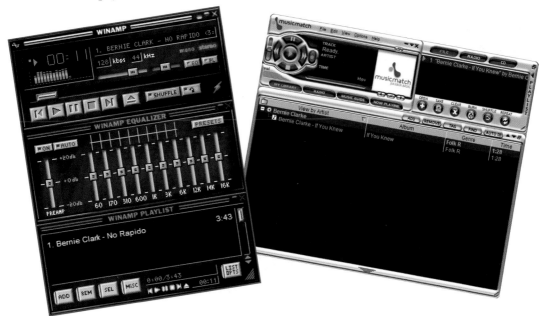

Many companies offer more than one version of their player. For example, several of the freeware and shareware players can be upgraded to more full-featured commercial versions. For most users, the free version is a good choice, although you may want to choose the commercial version for its increased functionality. Most music-player Web sites have a chart that compares the features of each version of its player.

To help you decide which player is right for you, Table 5-2 compares several of today's most popular digital music players, noting which ones support playback, encoding, CD burning, and streaming audio, as well as which file formats are supported by each player. You can download the freeware version of each these programs from its manufacturer's Web site. You'll learn more about the freeware version of each player in the following sections.

 For more information on where you can find media player Web sites, see the table at the end of this chapter.

 To learn more about features of popular media players, go to the CD-ROM segment *Media Player Software*.

Table 5-2 Popular digital music software.

Software Supported	Playback	Encoding (Ripping)	CD Burning	Streaming Audio	Formats
Liquid Player	Yes	Yes	Yes	Yes	AAC, LQT, MP3, WAV, WMA
MusicMatch® Jukebox	Yes	Yes	Yes	Yes	AVI, MP3, LQT, WAV, WMA
RealOne Player	Yes	Yes	Yes	Yes	AAC, LQT, MP3, RA, RM, WAV, WMA
Winamp	Yes	No	No	No	MIDI, MP3, WAV, WMA
Windows Media Player	Yes	Yes	Yes	Yes	AVI, MIDI, MP3 (playback only), WAV, WMA

 As you can see, not all players support all file formats. This means if you want to be able to play back and encode files in several different formats, you may need to use two or more separate programs.

Windows Media Player

As mentioned earlier, Windows Media Player is a versatile audio/video player that Microsoft includes with Windows 98 and later. If your computer runs either of these programs, you already have a copy of Windows Media Player at your disposal.

 For a more detailed exploration of the interface and key features of the Windows Media Player, go to the Web segment *Software Interface* within the Windows Media Player lesson.

You can use Windows Media Player to play back audio files in the MP3, WMA, WAV, MIDI, and other formats, organize playlists, and view information about the song you're playing. In addition, Windows Media Player can be used to rip files from audio CDs and, using the WMA format, make custom CDs. Figure 5-1 shows the Windows Media Player Interface.

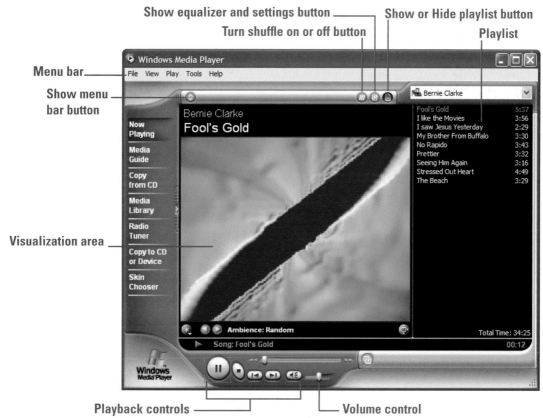

Figure 5-1 The Windows Media Player interface.

 To practice customizing the look and feel of the Windows Media Player, go to the Web segment *Visualizations: Customizing* within the Windows Media Player lesson.

MusicMatch Jukebox

MusicMatch Jukebox is a favorite among listeners thanks to its many features. For example, using the freeware version of MusicMatch Jukebox, you can play many of the most popular digital music formats, including MP3 and WMA and organize your music files into playlists. If you tire of your own music files, you can use MusicMatch Jukebox to listen to any number of Internet radio stations. Using this program, you can also encode new digital audio files in MP3 format (unlike Windows Media Player, MusicMatch Jukebox has built-in MP3 encoding, meaning there's nothing extra to add), and create custom CDs. In addition, you can use MusicMatch Jukebox to transfer your music files to any portable players you might have.

The MusicMatch interface consists of three separate windows—the Player, the Playlist, and My Library. (You can, however, change My Library to display the Music Guide on the MusicMatch Web site.) All three windows are displayed together, as shown in Figure 5-2.

 The My Library is an area of MusicMatch that you use to organize your music files. It provides the artist name, album, genre, and length of the song.

You can also dock or undock these windows and move them to fit your needs. All you do is click the **Dock** button in the corner of the window you want to dock or undock.

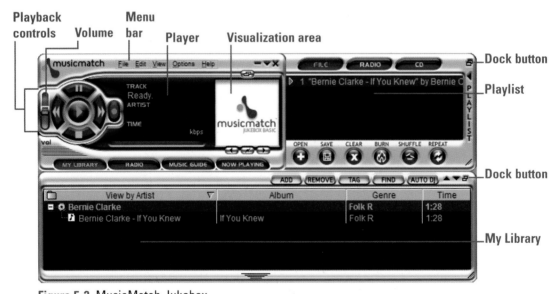

Figure 5-2 MusicMatch Jukebox.

 To learn how to download visualizations over the Web using MusicMatch, go to the Web segment *Visualizations: Downloading* within the MusicMatch Jukebox lesson.

To explore the interface and features of MusicMatch Jukebox, go to the Web segment *Software Interface* within the MusicMatch Jukebox lesson.

Winamp

Unlike Windows Media Player and MusicMatch Jukebox, you can't use Winamp to rip digital audio files from music CDs or make custom audio CDs. Winamp simply enables you to play back your music files. As a dedicated digital music player, however, Winamp (shown in Figure 5-3) is one of the most popular because it's been around for a long time—and you can get it free by downloading it from the Internet.

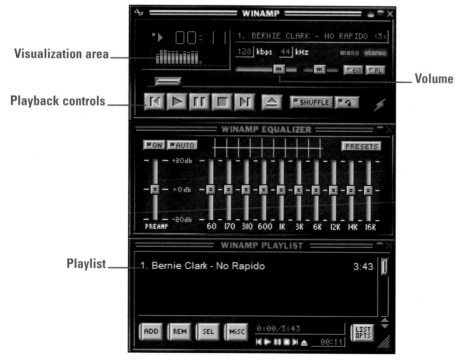

Figure 5-3 Winamp interface.

RealOne

Although you can use RealNetwork's RealOne to play and encode digital audio (and video) in many popular file formats, its real strength is that it enables you to play RealAudio and RealMedia streaming media files—the most popular formats for streaming media on the Web. For this reason, RealOne, which combines the capabilities of RealNetworks' RealPlayer and RealJukebox into one program, is among the most popular players on the market. Figure 5-4 shows the RealOne interface.

 You'll learn more about streaming media in Chapter 6.

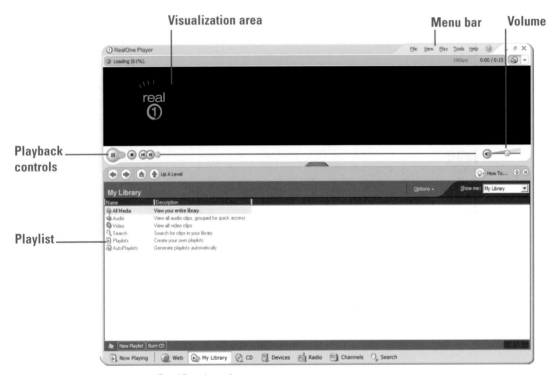

Figure 5-4 RealOne interface.

Liquid Player

Liquid Audio's Liquid Player (shown in Figure 5-5) enables you to play digital audio in several formats, including CDA, MP3, WMA, WAV, and LQT formats. In fact, the Liquid Player is one of the few digital music players that can play files in LQT format, which, as noted earlier in this chapter, is used by many music companies to distribute songs by their best-selling artists. In addition, Liquid Player can be used to encode digital music in either the MP3 or AAC format, and to make custom CDs (though not with LQT files).

Figure 5-5 Liquid Player interface.

Other Types of Players

Some digital music players do more than just play digital audio files. For example, several of the players discussed in the preceding sections, including Windows Media Player and MusicMatch Jukebox, are referred to as all-in-one players, because they enable you to record your own digital music files in addition to playing them back. In addition to those programs mentioned, you can choose from several commercial players that offer increased functionality over the basic features, such as faster CD burning and ripping.

Another type of player is a DJ mixer, which is a digital music player designed especially for DJ use—complete with advanced audio-mixing functions such as cross-fading and pitch change. DJs use these programs to combine songs into long playlists, insert transitions between songs, and automatically adjust the playback volume. With some programs, DJ's can even play songs backward and insert simulated vinyl-scratching effects.

Most of these programs are commercial software, which means you can't get them for free. Many, however, do have a shareware option, enabling you to try before you buy.

 To find more information about other types of players, see the table at the end of this chapter.

Downloading and Installing a Music Player

You've studied the various players and determined which one is right for you. You've even decided which version of the program you want to use. If you don't already have the player on your computer, it's time to download it and install it so you can enjoy the benefits of listening to digital music.

Fortunately, downloading a digital music player is an easy process. First, simply access the player's Web site. Then, navigate to the link titled "Download" or something similar, click it, and follow the instructions that appear. For example, Figure 5-6 shows the download page for the MusicMatch player.

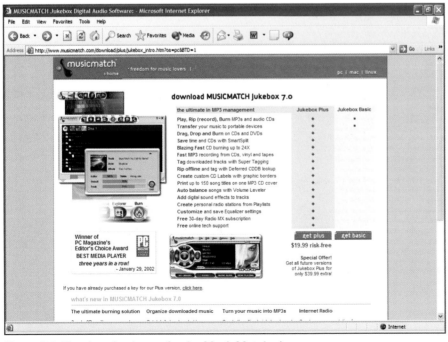

Figure 5-6 The download page for the MusicMatch player.

The specific instructions for downloading a player vary from program to program. Simply follow the prompts, and you'll be fine.

Some players try to install automatically when you download them (however, you always have a choice as to whether to run the installation). Others require you to save an installation file to your hard disk, and then run the file to install the software. To run the installation file, simply double-click its shortcut icon.

The first thing most installation routines do is ask you to read and accept a user agreement. If you want to be able to use the program, you must accept the terms of this agreement. Some programs install themselves automatically from here, whereas others ask you a series of questions to complete installation. For example, you might be asked to provide some information about yourself, such as your name and e-mail address, to register your software with the program's manufacturer (a step that is usually optional). Alternatively, you might be asked what type of Internet connection your system uses. When the installation routine is complete, you may need to reboot your computer. After you do, you're ready to use the player.

More About . . . Registering Your Player

As mentioned, you may be asked to register your software during the installation process. In most cases, however, registration is optional; that is, you can continue to use the player even if you don't register. Even if registering is optional, you might decide that doing so is a good idea because by registering, you're notified about software updates and special offers.

5

Using Your Digital Music Player

Now that you've chosen the digital music player you want to use, downloaded it from the Internet, and installed it on your machine, you're finally ready to use the player to listen to and record music files. Before you can use your digital music player, however, you must first start it.

 You'll learn how to burn CDs using your music files in Chapter 7.

In most cases, an icon for your music player was added to the All Programs menu of your start menu when the player was installed on your computer. In addition, some installation routines automatically add a shortcut icon for the player on your desktop. Once your player is up and running, you can use it to enjoy your music.

Whichever digital music player you use—be it Windows Media Player, MusicMatch Jukebox, Winamp, or what have you—you follow the same general steps to play a digital audio file. First, you select the song you want to play, either click **File** and choose **Open** or select the song in a playlist. Then, click the **Play** button to start the playback.

You should note that the playback controls for nearly every digital music player mimic those found on most CD players. For example, Windows Media Player's playback controls, shown here, feature a Play/Pause button, a Stop button, a Previous button, and a Next button.

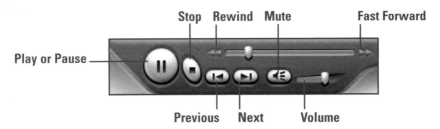

The following sections outline the use of Windows Media Player to play music files, record your own digital music files, and organize the music files on your computer. We chose Windows Media Player as our example because it comes preinstalled on Windows XP. That means there's a good chance it's already on your system too.

 Microsoft has released several versions of Windows Media Player over the years, so the version you have on your computer may look or work slightly differently from version shown in this chapter. The good news is that you can always upgrade to the most recent version of Windows Media Player from the Microsoft Web site.

Recording Digital Audio Files Using Windows Media Player

Of course, you can't play any digital music files on your hard drive if there aren't any there. Fortunately, Windows Media Player enables you to copy the music files on audio CDs to your hard drive. By default, Windows Media Player uses the WMA format, but you can also choose the format and quality you want to use for your ripped files. If you've installed the MP3 Creation Pack, you'll also have the added option of encoding to an MP3 file. First, open Windows Media Player by clicking the **start** menu, choosing **All Programs**, and choosing **Windows Media Player**.

To set the encoding format and quality level, do the following:

❶ Click the **Tools** menu and click **Options**.

❷ In the Options dialog box, click the **Copy Music** tab.

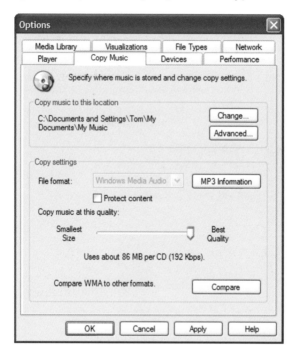

❸ In the Copy settings section, click the **File Format** drop-down list and choose either **Windows Media** or **MP3**. (Unless you've installed the MP3 Creation Pack, this drop-down list will be unavailable.)

❹ Unless you want to copy-protect the files you're ripping, uncheck the **Protect content** option. (This option is available only for Windows Media files.)

❺ Adjust the **Copy music at this quality** slider to set the sampling rate for your ripped files. Move the slider to the left for smaller files and lower sound quality, or to the right for larger files and higher sound quality. This can be adjusted for most file formats.

❻ Click **OK**.

You can start encoding the files on your audio CD by copying them to your hard drive. Here's how:

 If you want to include information about the songs you're copying, such as the name of the album and the artist, make sure you're connected to the Internet before you encode the files from your CD. Otherwise, Windows Media Player won't be able to download this information.

❶ Insert the CD you want to copy into your computer's CD-ROM drive.

❷ Click the **Copy from CD** button on the left side of the Windows Media Player window. The contents of the CD are displayed. If you can't see the names of the CD, click the **Get Names** button.

❸ Make sure that the tracks you want to copy are checked, and uncheck those tracks you *don't* want to copy.

4 Click the **Copy Music** button in the upper-right corner of the Windows Media Player window. Windows Media Player copies the selected tracks to your hard drive. The status is displayed in the Copy Status area as a progress bar that goes from pending to copying to copied.

 If copyright protection is enabled the first time you click Copy Music, a message appears notifying you that you won't be able to copy protected or licensed tracks copied from CD's to another computer. Click **OK**, or clear the **Do not protect content** check box, and then click **OK**.

5 After the file is copied, the Copy Status area reads Copied to Library. At which point, you can access your Media Library and play the file from your hard drive rather than from the CD.

 Unless you specify another folder, Windows Media Player copies the music files into your My Music folder. First, however, Windows Media Player creates a subfolder for the artist and, within the artist folder, another subfolder for this CD. If you would like to change to another folder in which to save your music use the Copy Music tab of the Options dialog box (see step 2 in the previous exercise).

Using Windows Media Player to Play Digital Music

To use Windows Media Player to play a digital music file, do the following:

1 Click the **Now Playing** button on the left side of the Windows Media Player window.

② If you can't see the File menu, move your pointer over the top of the player to see the menu bar. To play a file stored on your computer's hard drive, click **File** and choose **Open**.

 To load a music file from the Web instead of one stored on your computer, click **File** and choose **Open URL**.

③ In the Open dialog box, navigate to the folder in which the file you want to play is located. On most computers, digital music files are stored in the My Music folder. To open this folder, click the **My Documents** folder in the Look in drop-down list, and then click the **My Music** folder.

 If you have subfolders that contain the music you want to listen to, open the appropriate folder.

④ Select the music file you want to listen to.

⑤ Click the **Open** button.

⑥ Windows Media Player plays the selected file automatically. Use the playback controls to pause or stop play, or adjust the volume.

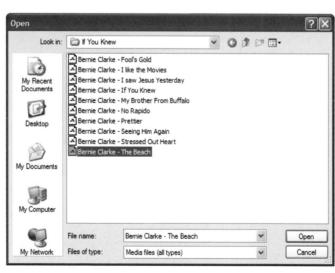

5

Stopping and Starting Playback

Once the music starts playing, you can use the other playback controls, shown here, to pause, stop, and restart the song. Click **Pause** to temporarily pause the playback. Click **Play** to restart the playback. Click **Stop** to completely halt the playback. In addition, most digital music players also have Previous and Next buttons. Click them to skip forward to the next track, or backward to the last song played.

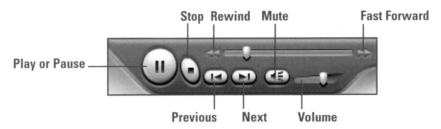

Adjusting the Volume

Most digital music players prominently display a volume control near the main controls. You use this control, generally a slider, to change the playback volume. Use your mouse pointer to drag the slider to the right and left (or up and down) to increase or decrease the volume.

Of course, you can also change your computer's volume with Windows volume controls. In Windows XP, open **Control Panel** and select **Sounds, Speech, and Audio Devices** and select **Adjust the system volume**. Then adjust the volume with the slider in the Sound and Audio Devices Properties dialog box. You can also double-click the **Volume** icon in the Windows system tray, on the far-right end of your taskbar, if available.

In addition, you can just adjust the volume using the volume controls on the actual speakers.

 It's probably best to set the volume on your music player at its highest level, and use the Windows volume control as your primary volume control.

Working with the Windows Media Player Media Library

The Windows Media Player Media Library enables you to collect all media content available on your computer and display it in one easy-to-use window. You can use your Windows Media Player Media Library to view music files on your computer, add files, sort them, play them, and organize them into playlists. To view the Media Library, simply click the **Media Library** button on the left side of the Windows Media Player window.

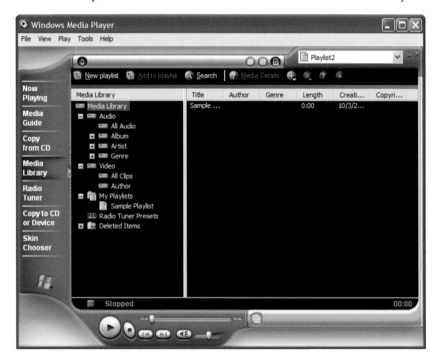

 Libraries and playlists are discussed in more detail in Chapter 6.

Searching Your Hard Drive for Audio Files

Once the Media Library window is open, you can quickly search your hard drive for audio (and video) files, and then add those files to the Media Library. Here's how:

❶ Click **Tools** and click **Search for Media Files**. The Search for Media Files dialog box opens.

There are other options you can choose in the Search for Media Files dialog box. Just click the **Advanced** button to expand it and select the Advanced search options you want to use.

2 Click **Search**. The Media Library locates the files and another Search for Media Files dialog box opens, displays a Progress bar, and then finally, the results of the search.

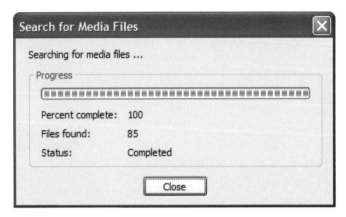

3 Click the **Close** button on both of the Search for Media Files dialog boxes.

4 Now all media files appear under the appropriate entries in the Media Library. For example, select **Audio**, and then **All Audio** and all audio files you have on your computer will be shown.

5 In the right side of the window, if you can't see the file you want to play, use the scroll bars to navigate until you can see the file. Double-click the file, or select the file and press play to play the file.

Adding Tracks to Your Media Library

You can also add tracks to your Media Library one at a time. For example, to add a single file on your hard drive to the Media Library, do the following:

1 Click **File**, click **Add to Media Library**, and click **Add File**.

2 The Open dialog box opens. Navigate to and select the file you want to add.

3 Click **Open**. The file is added to the Media Library window.

 Alternatively, you can drag a file in Windows Explorer and drop it in the Media Library window to add it to your Media Library. Even simpler, double-click a media file in Windows Explorer to play it; Media Library automatically adds it to its list of files.

If you want to add a song on the Internet to your Media Library, do the following:

1 Click **File**, click **Add to Media Library**, and click **Add URL**.

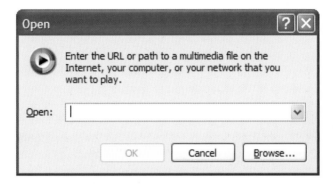

2 Enter the URL for the file you want to add to your Media Library and click **OK**. The file is added.

More About . . . Media Details

In Windows Media Player, if you have a bunch of songs that don't have the artist or album name, you can select those songs and click the Media Details button to update the information from the Internet. Alternatively, you can right-click the song and choose **Edit** to fill in the information manually. That way, you don't have a bunch of songs with an unknown artist or album title.

 To learn more about organizing and adding files to your media library using Windows Media Player, go to the Web segment *Media Collection: Organizing* within the Windows Media Player lesson.

To learn how to create and add to a music library with MusicMatch, go to the Web segment *Music Library: Creating* within the MusicMatch Jukebox lesson.

Sorting Music Files in the Media Library

Before long, you may end up with dozens or even hundreds of music files in your Media Library. Sifting through all those files to find the ones you want can be taxing. Fortunately, the Media Library enables you to sort your music files using the following categories:

- ✦ Title

- ✦ Artist

- ✦ Album

- ✦ Composer

- ✦ Genre

- ✦ Length

To sort your files, simply click the header atop the column by which you want to sort. For example, to list files by artist, click the Artist column heading. In addition, you can resize the columns by putting your mouse pointer over the line next to the column title (your pointer will change shape like the one in the figure below) and dragging it to the size you want.

To instruct Windows Media Player to go online to the Windows Media Database to update track information, thereby enabling you to more accurately sort your music files, select the **Album** entry in the left pane, right-click an album title, and choose **Update Names**.

Playing Songs from Within the Media Library

Once you've used Media Library to locate the song you want to hear, actually playing it is a snap. To do so, simply double-click the song's file name and the song is played. Alternatively, you can select the song and click the play button.

Using Your Media Library to Create Playlists

If you're like most people, you enjoy several different kinds of music. For example, when you're feeling mellow, you might prefer to listen to classical music. If you're feeling energized, however, hip-hop might be your genre of choice. No matter what type of music you enjoy, playlists enable you to organize your music files into groups. For example, you might place all your music files that contain songs from your youth into a playlist called "Songs from the past." Then, you can opt to play the files in the playlist either in the order in which they're listed or randomly.

 To know the steps in creating and editing a music playlist with MusicMatch, go to the Web segment *Playlist Management* within the MusicMatch Jukebox lesson.

To be able to create a playlist with Windows Media Player, go to the Web segment *Playlist: Creating* within the Windows Media Player lesson.

5

Creating a new playlist couldn't be simpler. Just do the following:

❶ Click the **New Playlist** button in the upper-left corner of the Media Library window.

❷ The New Playlist dialog box opens. Type a name for the playlist and click **OK**.

Once you've created a playlist, you simply add the files you want it to contain. Here's how:

❶ In the Media Library window, click a file you want to add to your playlist to select it.

In Windows Media Player, as in most music players, you can select multiple files by holding down the **CTRL** key as you click on the files you want to add.

❷ Drag the file(s) to the desired playlist under My Playlists on the left side of your Media Library window, as shown here.

To listen to an entire playlist, simply double-click it under My Playlists on the left side of your Media Library window. The songs in the Playlist play in order by default. To shuffle them—that is, play them in a random order—click the **Turn shuffle on** button.

Turn shuffle on or off button

Changing Views in Windows Media Player

Just as you can resize most program windows, you can resize the player on your desktop—and, with some players, display less information and fewer controls. For example, Windows Media Player enables you display either the full player or a compact version that shrinks or hides some lesser-used controls.

To switch to Skin mode (which is compact mode), simply click the **Switch to skin mode** button on the bottom center of the Windows Media Player window, or click the **View** menu and click **Skin Mode**.

Switch to skin mode button

When Windows Media Player is in Skin mode, a small window appears at the bottom-right of the desktop. You can click the window to choose to return to Full mode or to open a new file.

 Unlike Windows Media Player, MusicMatch Jukebox displays different parts of the program in different windows. You can resize or move each window individually, or close any windows that aren't important to your current task.

Applying a New Skin to Your Windows Media Player Program Window

If you're the kind of person who enjoys applying wallpaper to your computer desktop or choosing your own screensavers, you'll appreciate the ability to change the *skins* on your digital music player. Doing so alters the look and feel of your player's controls and interface by varying the textures, colors, and fonts used.

Many digital music players, including Windows Media Player and MusicMatch Jukebox, support the use of skins. In fact, both Windows Media Player and MusicMatch Jukebox ship with several skins pre-installed. If none of the pre-installed skins appeals to you, you can download more from each manufacturer's Web site. Just look for a link that says skins or if the site has a search utility, search for skins. For example, in Windows Media Player, click the **More Skins** button, which opens the Windows Media Web site where you can download more skins.

To change skins in Windows Media Player, do the following:

❶ Click the **Skin Chooser** button on the left side of the Windows Media Player window.

2 Click a skin in the list on the left side of the window, and preview it in the right-hand pane.

3 Continue clicking skins until you find one you like.

④ To apply the skin, click **Apply Skin**. As shown here, once you've changed its skin, Windows Media Player looks completely different.

TO KEEP ON LEARNING . . .

Go to the CD-ROM and select the segment:

✦ *Media Player Software* to learn more about features of popular media players.

Go online to **www.LearnwithGateway.com** and log on to select:

✦ *MusicMatch Jukebox*

✦ *Windows Media Player*

✦ *Internet Links and Resources*

   ✦ *Digital Music File Formats*

   ✦ *Digital Music Player Software*

   ✦ *Other Types of Music Players*

✦ *FAQs*

With the *Survive & Thrive* series, refer to *Communicate and Connect to the Internet* for more information on:

✦ *Downloading from the Internet*

Refer to *Use and Care for Your PC* for more information on:

✦ *Using your CD/DVD drive*

Gateway offers a hands-on training course that covers many of the topics in this chapter. Additional fees may apply. Call **888-852-4821** for enrollment information. If applicable, please have your customer ID and order number ready when you call.

CHAPTER 6

Exploring Music on the Web

96   Understanding Online Music Formats
Your digital music player matches your needs

98   Finding Music Online
Search the Web for your favorite songs

105   Downloading Digital Music Files
Obtain audio tracks from the Internet

107   Using Online Databases
Find music information online

110   Organizing Your Music
Manage your library of digital audio files

113   Exploring Internet Radio
Listen to live broadcasts in real-time

119   Sharing Your Digital Music
Review file-sharing options

125   Keeping Your System Secure
Ward off viruses and avoid other security pitfalls

When it comes to finding music online, there's good news and bad news. The good news is that the Internet boasts literally hundreds of Web sites that offer digital audio file downloads, each with its own unique selection of music. That means that no matter how obscure the song you seek or how unknown its performer, chances are you'll find it on the Internet.

Now, the bad news: The Internet boasts literally hundreds of Web sites that offer digital audio file downloads, each with its own unique selection of music. That means actually finding the song you want may involve sifting through dozens of sites.

Here, you'll learn about several online music sites that you can visit to search for your favorite digital music. You'll find out how to download and listen to that music. You'll even discover a new and interesting way to listen to digital music: streaming audio. Finally, you'll learn how to organize your music files so you can easily find the ones you need, and how to keep your system safe from the viruses and other problems that can result from downloading files over the Internet.

Understanding Online Music Formats

Before you locate and download music files, you'll want to remember that your computer's digital music software or your portable playback device is limited in the types of music files it can play. For this reason, you'll want to be certain the music files you download from the Web use a format your equipment can read. (You learned about the various file formats in Chapter 5.) Fortunately, most of the music files you encounter on the Web will be MP3 files, which just about every music player can handle. However, some subscription sites might offer files in WMA, LQT, or AAC format.

Alternatively, as you search for music on the Internet, you may find all the tracks on entire CDs within a single file, typically with a ZIP extension. A ZIP file acts similarly to a folder—that is, it may hold several files within it. Unlike a folder, however, a ZIP file compresses each file it contains. Before you can play the music files in a downloaded ZIP file, you need to extract them, which is the process of removing them from the ZIP file and decompressing them.

To do so using Windows XP, follow these steps:

1 Open My Computer.

2 Navigate to the folder in which the ZIP file is stored.

3 Right-click the ZIP file's icon and choose **Extract All** from the shortcut menu that appears.

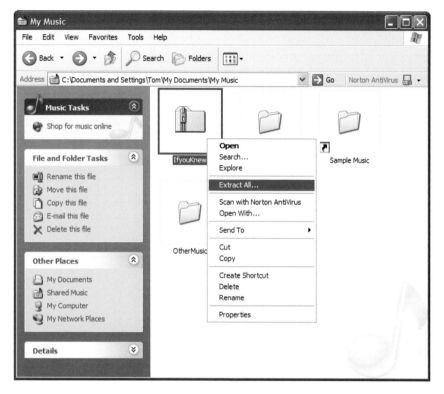

4 The Extraction Wizard appears. Click **Next**.

5 Select the destination folder where you want the extracted files to be deposited. The default folder is displayed. Use the Browse button to select another folder. Click **Next**.

6 Click **Finish**. A new window displaying the extracted contents opens.

Each music file in the ZIP file is copied to the indicated folder. Depending on who did the zipping, you might even find a graphics file containing the CD artwork!

Finding Music Online

The Internet is a vast network of computers that stores billions and billions of files. And chances are, one of those computers houses the very music file you need to complete your collection. The burning question is, how do you find that computer?

In this section, you'll learn about several online music sites that you can visit to search for your favorite digital music. Some sites, called *digital audio archives,* offer lots of music for free. Other sites, called *subscription music services,* charge a monthly fee. Still others (discussed later in this chapter) enable you to connect with other users to swap your own personal files.

 Remember to add any music sites you like to your Web browser's Favorites list for easy access later.

Each online site differs in the way it enables you to search for music. That is, you perform a specific set of steps to locate music on one site, and a completely different set of steps to find music on another. We suggest that you consult each site's online help information for specific information about locating the music you want.

 Many of the Web sites mentioned in this publication are independent sites not affiliated with Gateway. We've recommended them because we thought they would be of interest; however, Gateway cannot guarantee the accuracy or safety of another person or company's Web site.

Using Digital Audio Archives

The first place to look online for digital music is at one of the many online digital audio archives. These sites typically offer large databases of music files (most in MP3 format) contributed by other site visitors. In most cases, you can search these digital audio archive sites by artist, song title, or by genre.

As you learned in Chapter 3, most major record companies don't license their copyrighted music for free distribution on the Web. For this reason, many online digital audio archives specialize in presenting new artists and independent music. This provides a great way for upcoming artists to gather a following of fans. For example, the MP3.com site is a great place to find downloadable music by newer and independent artists.

Just open the home page and start digging around the same way you would at a record store.

6

If you're looking for a particular song, but don't have time to check several digital audio archives one at a time, you might want to visit any of several sites that function as search engines for music stored on other sites. These sites enable you to search many digital audio archives and other music sites at once for audio files in the format(s) you specify. Musicseek is a site that allows you to search many other sites at once for music in the format(s) you specify.

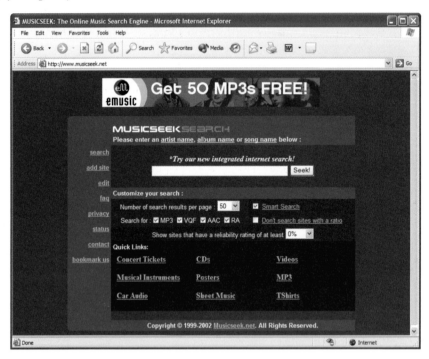

Just type an artist name, album name, or song name in the search field, click the **Seek** button, and a list of results appears.

If you still can't find the information you're looking for, try visiting an online store that sells CDs. At these online stores you can shop from the convenience of your own home. Many stores provide sample digital music clips you can download to preview CDs before you buy them.

 To visit some of the digital audio archives, music search sites, and online stores we've found on the Web, see the table at the end of this chapter.

Using Subscription Music Services

Understandably, record companies and their artists want to get paid for the music they provide. For this reason, they license their music to Web sites that collect money from users who download it. These Web sites are called *subscription music services.* In most cases, users who subscribe to such services pay a monthly fee in exchange for the right to download a certain number of songs each month to their computer. In addition, some free downloads, typically for promotional purposes, may also be available.

 If you decide to subscribe to a music service, be sure you carefully read the membership agreement first. As mentioned, some services limit how many files you can download each month. In addition, you may be limited in what you can do with those files. For example, some sites won't let you burn their downloaded files to CD. Finally, be aware that most music subscription sites distribute music using file formats other than MP3, which is very versatile. For example, WMA files, which have built-in licensing features, are commonly used. Make sure your computer's digital music player or portable player can handle the file format used by the subscription service.

These subscription sites are, in general, very easy to use, but typically offer only those songs released by a particular record company. This means if you're a real music junkie, you might want to subscribe to more than one service. There are many to choose from; read on for information about the following subscription sites:

✦ EMusic

✦ MusicNet®

✦ press*play*™

✦ RealOne™

 Because the Internet is a constantly evolving environment, some of the sites we discuss in the following section may change. To find out where you can get more information, see the table at the end of this chapter.

6

EMusic

Unlike most subscription services, which limit the number of downloads you can perform each month, subscribing to the EMusic service affords you unlimited MP3 file downloads for a single monthly fee. This service, which features known artists from more than 900 independent record labels, offers more than 200,000 music files in its database. Using the service, you can download either individual songs or complete albums. Finding the songs you want is simple. You can search by title or artist, or you can browse through music by category.

MusicNet

MusicNet, a joint venture between AOL Time Warner (which owns the Warner Music Group), Bertelsmann (which owns BMG Entertainment), the EMI Group, and RealNetworks, offers music from the Warner, EMI, and Zomba record labels. Unlike most other subscription services, however, MusicNet doesn't offer its service directly to consumers. Instead, it licenses its technology and music database to other Web sites as the engine for their music services. Napster and RealOne are some of the companies that use MusicNet.

pressplay

The press*play* partnership between Sony, Universal Music, and Yahoo! offers subscription music services featuring Sony and Universal artists. Like MusicNet, press*play* licenses its technology to other sites, including MP3.com, MSN®, and Roxio™ (see Figure 6-1). Therefore, you access the consumer version through software or services such as Roxio and MP3.com, respectively.

Figure 6-1 The press*play* subscription service, via Roxio.

The consumer version of press*play*, offers digital music for downloading and streaming audio. Subscriptions range from Basic to Platinum. The different subscription levels determine how much music you can access. Specifically, the Basic level limits you to 30 downloads per month, whereas the Platinum level allows you as many as 100 downloads.

 If you normally buy several CDs a month, you should consider signing up for the higher levels of service at any of these subscription services. Also, you might want to consider signing up for several subscription services.

You can make CDs from the press*play* songs you download, although press*play* limits the number of songs you can copy. You're also limited to copying just one song per artist per CD, which means you can make compilation CDs, but not complete single-artist CDs.

RealOne

As mentioned previously, the RealOne subscription music service from Real Networks uses the MusicNet platform. This means when you use RealOne, you'll find music in all formats for artists signed to the Warner, EMI, and Zomba labels. In addition, RealOne offers streaming audio and Internet radio content, as well video content, including news broadcasts, televised sporting events, and more.

 You can listen to the songs you download from RealOne on your computer, but you can't burn (copy) downloaded songs onto compact discs. Also, unlike the files you download from a digital music archive site, the songs you download from RealOne expire after 30 days. To play a song that's expired, you must reactivate it—which consumes one of your download credits for the new month.

Like press*play*, RealOne offers different levels of subscription from Basic to Gold. Gold members can download more music than Basic users (125 downloads per month), and can access premium Internet radio content.

You can access RealOne content using RealOne Player, as shown in Figure 6-2. This digital music player handles everything from simple audio downloads to streaming video Webcasts. It works best with a broadband connection (typically a cable modem or DSL for home users).

Figure 6-2 The RealOne subscription service, accessed via the RealOne Player.

Other Subscription Services

Several other subscription music services are worth checking out. Subscription services offer access to major-label artists that often don't permit free archives to store their music.

 To visit some of the online Music subscription, record label and artists sites we've found on the Web, see the table at the end of this chapter.

Downloading Digital Music Files

Once you've found the song you want, downloading it to your computer is the next step. When you *download* a digital music file, you simply copy it to your computer from another computer on the Web. When your computer receives the file, it stores it on your hard disk. Once the file is there, you can listen to it anytime you want.

The specific instructions for downloading audio files differ from site to site, but most sites prominently display a Download (or similarly named) link or button alongside when you locate a music file on the site. Simply click this button, specify where on your hard disk you want to store the downloaded file, and then click **Save**. Assuming your computer uses a standard 56.6 Kbps modem to connect to the Internet, downloading a typical 3 minute song in the MP3-format takes about 10 to 15 minutes. (The same file downloads in only a minute or two if you have a cable or DSL connection.)

 To learn more about the steps and issues of downloading music from the Internet, go to the CD-ROM segment *Music Files: Downloading*.

For our example, we're going to download a music file from **www.gateway.com/learningdownloads** using Internet Explorer on Windows XP. To download and play the song named "If You Knew," follow these steps:

❶ Click **start** and choose **Internet** to open your browser.

6

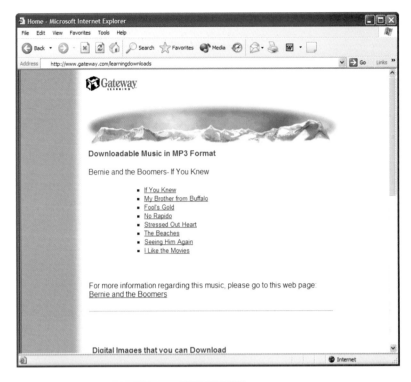

2 Type this URL into the Address field: **www.gateway.com/ learningdownloads**.

3 Click **Go** or press **ENTER**. The Downloadable Music in MP3 Format site opens.

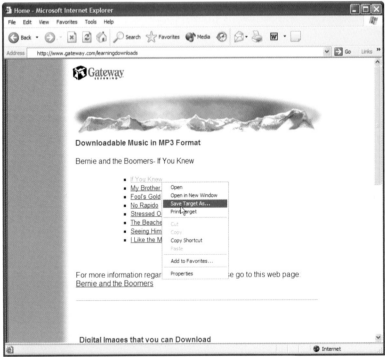

4 Right-click the **If You Knew link**, and then choose **Save Target As**.

When you click on a link and hear music immediately or after a few seconds, you're initiating a stream of the music instead of a download.

5 The Save As dialog box opens. Use this dialog box to select the destination download folder. You can also elect to change the file name of the audio file being downloaded. Click **Save** to initiate the download to the designated folder.

 A common download destination folder is the My Music folder located within My Documents. Be sure you pick a destination folder that you will remember.

After you download the file, you use a digital music player—such as Windows Media Player or MusicMatch Jukebox—to play the music through your computer. (Review Chapter 5 for information about playing music files.)

It's also possible to download video and audio files using Windows Media Player. By selecting the **Media Guide** button, the WindowsMedia.com Web site is displayed within the Windows Media Player. Navigating this content is the same as navigating a Web browser. If you find something that interests, you just click to watch or listen to it streaming over the Internet or to download it to your computer.

Using Online Databases

When you play music using your digital music player, you typically see information about the song displayed somewhere in the player window. Typically, that information comes from an *online database,* which is a collection of information (in this case, CD information) stored on the Internet.

Most digital music players obtain this data from one of two online databases: CDDB® (CD database) or AMG (All-Music Guide). Both databases contain all sorts of information about compact-disc music. Such as the artist, CD title, song tracks, and so on. When you access a CD (or certain MP3 files) using a digital music player, the player connects to the Internet and pulls song, artist, and album information from one of the online databases, which the player then displays.

 Digital music players will search online CD databases when you insert a custom made audio CD but they won't display or find any information. The search is successful usually only for commercially produced audio CDs. In addition, if you're not currently connected to the Internet, most music players will attempt to launch your connection software and establish a connection with your Internet service provider or online service.

CDDB

Gracenote's™ CDDB is the world's largest database of audio CD and song titles, and is accessed by more than 28-million users each month. Several major subscription music services and many digital music players license CDDB for use with their services or software.

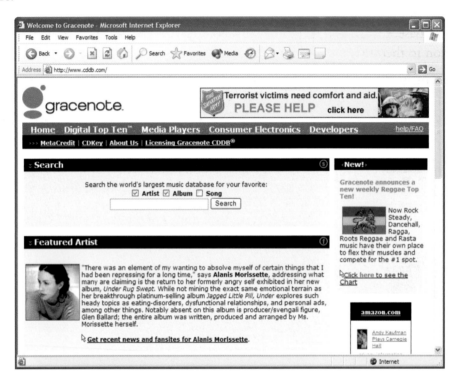

You can also access the CDDB database on your own to locate information about an artist, album, or song. Simply use your Web browser to open the site. Then, type the name of an artist, album, or song you want to research in the Search box and click **Search** or press **ENTER**. CDDB returns a list of matching CDs. Click a title to see the CD's track listing.

All Music Guide

CDDB's chief competitor is the AMG (All Music Guide), which collected information about recorded music and published it in book form long before the Internet was around. As with CDDB, many major subscription music services, as well as several digital music players, license AMG for use with their services or software. In fact, because the information in the AMG database is typically more comprehensive than that in the CDDB database, some services, license with both CDDB and AMG to provide information to their users.

Not surprisingly, you can also access AMG using your Web browser. Once there, you can search the 500,000+ albums in AMG's database by artist, album, song, genre, or record label. Results include album information, track information, and even detailed personnel listings.

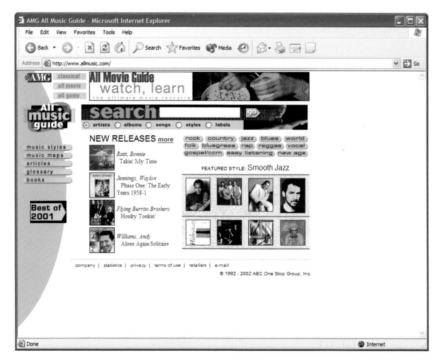

 AMG provides similar databases for movies (All Movie Guide) and video games (All Game Guide). You can access these sites from the main All Music Guide site. See the table at the end of this chapter to find out how to access the site. In addition, to find out where to go to visit some of the music database sites available on the Web, see the table at the end of this chapter.

Organizing Your Music

If you're a music lover, there's a good chance you have imposed a strict organizational structure on your CD-storage unit. Perhaps you alphabetize your CDs by artist, or arrange them by release date. Or maybe you've categorized your discs by genre or some other method. The point is, by organizing your discs, no matter which system you use, you can quickly locate the one you want to hear.

However, a computer's hard drive is vast, so unlike CDs that are typically stored in one location, music files can be anywhere in your computer. Fortunately, you can organize the music files on your computer making each music file easy to locate. There are several ways to do so: using Windows XP's folders, libraries and playlists, or professional music library-management software.

Storing Your Files Using Windows XP Folders

When you download a music file, most online music sites enable you to specify where on your hard drive the file should be saved. In most cases, the default location is the My Music folder. Likewise, if you use a digital music player to record files from a CD, the player probably copies them to the My Music folder by default. Some programs and sites, however, save files to their own special directories.

 When you copy an entire CD to the My Music folder, the CD cover art is also copied. As a result, when you open the My Music folder, you see the cover art for each CD in the folder.

The My Music folder is a good location to store your digital music files for a couple reasons. First, a lot of programs look in the My Music folder for music files by default. Second, Windows XP provides some useful digital music file-management tools in this folder in the Music Tasks panel. For example, you can play all the songs in a folder by clicking **Play all** in the Music Tasks panel. Alternatively, to launch your digital music player and play individual songs directly from the My Music folder, just double-click the file you want to hear.

Music Tasks panel —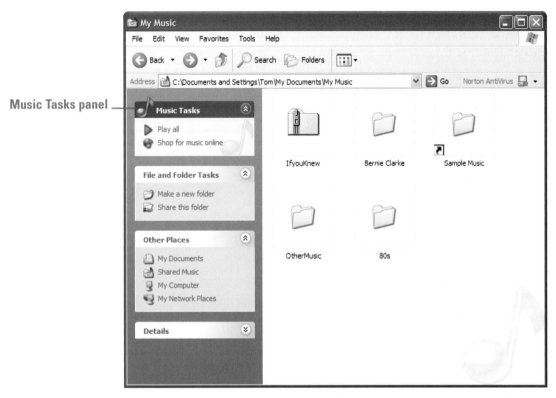

Of course, you can create subfolders in the My Music folder to better organize the files you download. For example, some users create subfolders for specific artists, albums, genres, or what have you.

 If you can't fit all your digital music files on your hard disk because it isn't large enough, you can store your files on removable Zip or Jazz drives, or on recordable CDs.

Working with Music Libraries and Playlists

If you're like most people, you enjoy several different kinds of music. For example, you might listen to jazz when you're feeling mellow, blues when you're feeling down, or rock and roll when you're feeling energized. You'll probably have your music stored in your My Music organized by genre, artist, and/or album using folders. But what if you want to play one song from one album, two from another, and then three from another genre?

Well, that's where libraries (sometimes called track pool, media library, or my library, depending on the software vendor) and playlists come in. A library keeps a record of all the media files on your system. In addition, it also stores several details regarding the media, including the title, album, artist, and where the media is stored on the computer. The software usually prompts you to scan your system for media upon installation or you can run the scan later. After the scan has completed, your library is stocked with an index of all the songs on your system. You can use this index to add songs to your playlists.

 When you delete media from a playlist, some applications prompt you as to whether you want to delete it from your computer as well. Unless you choose this option, when you delete items from your music library, you're not deleting them from your hard drive.

A *playlist* is an ordered listing of songs that you want to play. It's a bit like creating a custom tape or CD that only includes your favorite songs. For example, you might place all your music files

that contain songs from your youth into a playlist called "songs from the past." That way, when you want to play all those songs, you need not load each one individually. Instead, you simply load the playlist.

Chapter 5 demonstrates how to create and use playlists in Windows Media Player.

To learn more about music libraries and their uses, go to the CD-ROM segment *Media Libraries*.

Using Music-Management Software

Even though you can use most media players to manage your software, if you have many downloaded files, you might need a more powerful way to catalog all that digital music. If so, you'll be interested in learning about dedicated music management software. *Music management software* organizes and manages all the music on your hard disk. These programs help you catalog your library of downloaded music with more precision than you can with most digital music players. In many cases, you can also use these programs to manage your CDs, LPs, and cassette tapes.

All these programs give you the option to enter CD and song data manually, and many also link to CDDB or other online databases to obtain more complete information. For example, with Collectorz.com Music Collector, you "scan" a CD by inserting it in your computer's CD-ROM drive. The program adds the title to its database and inserts additional information obtained from CDDB.

To find out where you can get more information on the music management programs, see the table at the end of this chapter.

Exploring Internet Radio

There are two basic ways to play digital music you find on the Internet. The first requires you to download a complete digital audio file before you can open it in a digital music player and play it. The second method, steaming audio (sometimes called *Webcasting*), is used for playing back live radio broadcasts and other programs over the Web, or for offering previews of songs before you download them. You'll also find some music on the Web in the streaming-audio formats you read about in Chapter 5, although these are mostly used to broadcast live events.

All streaming-audio broadcasts on the Internet are informally called *Internet radio*.

With streaming audio, you don't save a file on your hard drive to listen to it. Instead, the music comes to you a little bit at a time as the player plays it, similar to the way you listen to an AM or FM station on your car radio. Streaming-audio players work by

6

playing the first part of the recording before they finish downloading the rest of the audio file. As shown in Figure 6-3, this process gathers the first part of the audio stream in a small buffer, or storage area on your hard disk. When the buffer is full the audio starts playing—while the player continues to download the rest of the song. As a result, streaming-audio files can begin playing almost immediately, eliminating the long wait associated with typical digital audio file downloads. And with live audio broadcasts, the streaming is continuous until the broadcast ends. Depending on the type of Webcast you're listening to, there may or may not be a file for it stored on your hard disk after the broadcast. If not, the audio stream can only be listened to once, in real time.

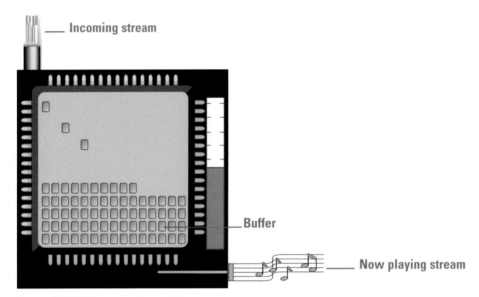

Figure 6-3 How streaming audio works.

 Some streaming-audio sites play their audio through your Web browser, using a streaming-audio *plug-in.* This is a small software program that attaches to your browser, and enables it to function like a streaming-audio player. If your browser needs a specific plug-in, you'll be prompted to download it from the Web site; the download and installation is typically fast and automatic.

In the following sections, you'll learn all about Internet radio, from the sound quality of streaming audio to the audio formats this technology uses. You'll also find out how to use an Internet radio player to listen to Internet radio, and discover some of the more popular Internet radio sites.

 To gain an understanding of the benefits and uses of Internet radio, go to the CD-ROM segment *Internet Radio.*

Understanding Sound Quality

Because streaming audio sends its signal through your Internet connection—and because most Internet connections are made via normal phone lines—the amount of information that can be streamed at one time is sometimes limited. This results in lower-quality sound than what you're used to with traditional digital music downloads. If you have a DSL or

cable modem connection, however, you can choose the "high speed" option for your streaming audio, which will provide higher-quality sound. The faster your connection speed, the better quality the sound you'll hear.

The quality of your Internet connection can also affect streaming-audio quality. If the connection between your computer and the streaming Web site gets interrupted or slows down, you'll hear it in the form of halting, shuttering playback. If you experience this type of playback, consider trying the site again during a less-congested time of day.

The best times of day to listen to streaming audio or download digital audio files are early in the morning, mid-day, and late at night. The worst times are right after school and in the early evening.

Understanding Streaming-Audio Formats

Streaming audio exists on the Web in two main established formats: RealNetworks' RealAudio and the Microsoft WMA (Windows Media Audio) formats. A third common format, which is a relative newcomer, is the streaming MP3 format. (Refer to Chapter 5 for more information about the various audio formats.)

You may occasionally encounter audio files with a .mov extension. This is the QuickTime® format, by Apple, used for both audio and video. You have to download the QuickTime player to watch or listen to these files.

RealAudio

RealNetworks established its leadership in the streaming-audio market when it introduced the RealAudio format back in 1994. It's still the most-used format for streaming audio. RealNetworks also developed a format for streaming video, called *RealMedia*. The RealMedia format works for both video and audio, so it's not unusual to see streaming-audio files with a .rm or .ram extension.

Windows Media Audio

RealAudio's chief streaming competitor is Microsoft's WMA format, which can be used for both traditional downloading and for streaming audio. WMA files are not as widely used as RealAudio files, although they provide similar performance quality. Microsoft's Windows Media format for video files also works for streaming audio. These files have either a .asf or .avi extension.

Streaming MP3

There's a recent addition to the world of streaming-audio formats. This one is based on the established MP3 format. In fact, this new format is the MP3 format—fed through a technology called *SHOUTcast*. SHOUTcast servers enable Web sites to stream regular MP3 files so listeners can start listening before the entire file is downloaded. Streaming MP3 files play through Winamp and many other popular digital music players. You can find list of SHOUTcast servers at the SHOUTcast Web site.

Selecting an Internet Radio Player

When it comes to playing streaming-audio files, your choice of player depends on the format of the file you want to listen to. For example, if you want to listen to a RealAudio file, you typically use the RealOne Player. To listen to a Windows Media Audio file, you typically use the Windows Media Player. Winamp is typically the player of choice for streaming MP3 files.

In Windows XP, if you click on a link to listen to a file in a particular format and you don't have a player that supports that format installed, you're prompted to use a Web service to find the appropriate program or to select a program from your existing programs.

Windows	[?][X]

Windows cannot open this file:

File: 20020322.me.01[1].ram

To open this file, Windows needs to know what program created it. Windows can go online to look it up automatically, or you can manually select from a list of programs on your computer.

What do you want to do?

⊙ Use the Web service to find the appropriate program

○ Select the program from a list

[OK]   [Cancel]

In this case, we're trying to download a RealAudio file and know we don't have it installed so we choose to use the Web service to locate the appropriate program. Internet Explorer then provides you with information on the file as well as where you can download the software you need to listen to the file.

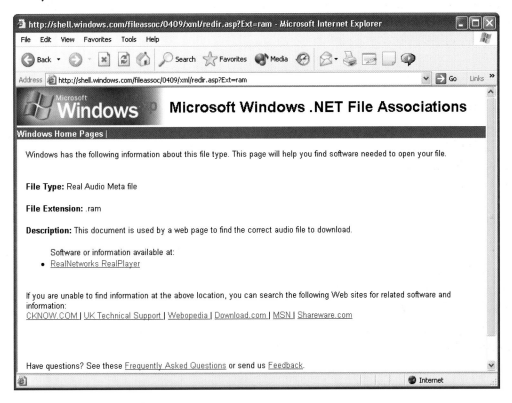

This isn't to say that these players are capable of playing only a single format. In fact, most players play multiple streaming formats. Most streaming broadcasts, however, use their format's default player when they start playing on your computer—so if you choose to play a RealAudio broadcast, chances are it will play through the RealOne Player.

Listening to Internet Radio

Internet radio content covers a broad range, from audio books to news broadcasts, from streamed CDs to live concerts. You'll also find a lot of real-world radio stations streaming on the Internet, making Internet radio a great way to listen to stations you can't pick up on your local AM or FM radio. To listen to Internet radio using your computer, just use your digital music player to dial into a station broadcasting music (or sports or talk shows) that you like. Click **Play** and leave the player running in the background as you work.

Have you ever heard a song on the radio and wondered what it was called or who sang it? If so, you'll appreciate the fact that many Internet radio stations display the title and performer of the song that is currently playing, right on your computer screen.

For example, to listen to Internet radio using Windows Media Player, follow these steps:

1 Click the **Radio Tuner** button on the left side of the Windows Media Player window. Windows Media Player connects to the WindowsMedia.com Web site, and displays a list of featured stations.

2 To see more stations, click a genre in the Find More Stations section or use the search box to search for specific types of music or station call letters.

3 When you find a station you like, click the station name to display more information and listening options.

4 Some stations can be listened to from within Windows Media Player. For these stations, click **Play** to begin listening the player shows a buffering activity while it pre-loads the first part of the streamed media. Other stations require you to visit their Web sites to listen. For these stations, click the **Visit Website** link, and follow the playback instructions on the site.

More About . . . Streaming Audio and Firewalls

If you want to listen to Internet radio at work, you may experience some difficulties. That's because many corporate networks use firewalls to protect against unwanted intrusions. (A *firewall* is a software program that blocks certain types of Internet traffic.) Unfortunately, firewalls can also block streaming-audio and -video Webcasts. If you find that Internet radio broadcasts are blocked, check with your network administrator to see if the firewall can be configured to allow streaming media to be received.

Internet Radio Sites

Several Web sites offer Internet radio broadcasts. Some of these sites offer Webcasts of traditional radio stations, whereas others offer Web-specific content, Echo is just one of the sites we found. Many Internet radio sites, such as Echo, enable you to create your own custom "stations" based on your listening preferences. For how-to information, check the site's help system.

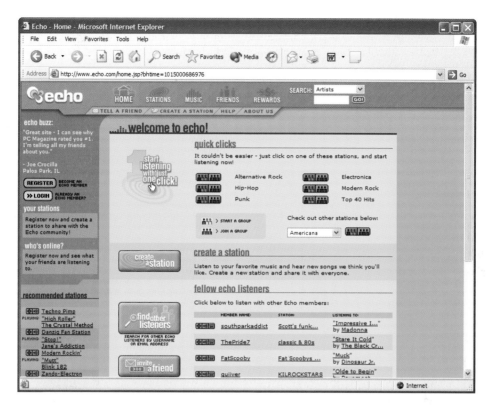

 To visit some of the Internet radio sites we've found on the Web, see the table at the end of this chapter.

Sharing Your Digital Music

If you can't find the music you want in a digital music archive or at a music-subscription service, you're not completely out of luck. Chances are there's another user, somewhere on the Internet, with a copy of the song you want. All you have to do is find that user.

When users swap digital audio files in this manner, it's called *P2P* (peer-to-peer) *file-sharing* because both computers are *peers.* That is, neither one functions as a central computer from which to download files. It's just you and another user, your *peer,* swapping files. When you search other users' computers for the music you want, you use a *P2P file-sharing service,* which enables users to connect to each other's computers to swap digital music files. In this section, you find out how peer-to-peer file sharing works and what services you can use to share files.

The big issue with file sharing, however, isn't technical—it's legal. Most songs you find online are copyrighted, and whether copyrighted material like this can be freely shared, without compensating the artist or copyright holder, is under debate. Some copyright holders don't want their songs shared online, and have taken legal action against various file-sharing services to remove their songs from circulation—or, in some instances, to shut down the file-sharing service itself. It's a complicated issue; you can read more about it in Chapter 3 of this book.

Understanding Peer-to-Peer File Sharing

Unlike a Web site, where files are stored on a central Web server and are available for downloading to your computer, a P2P file-sharing system is a network of personal computers. You connect to this network and search other users' computers for the files you want to download. When you find a match, you copy the file from that other user's computer to your computer, without any interaction with a central Web site.

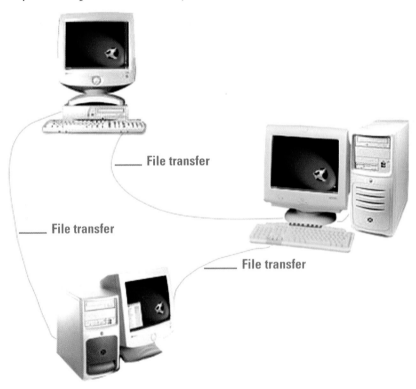

File transfer

File transfer

File transfer

 A *Web server* is a computer used to store and download files on the Internet.

Internet-based P2P file sharing became popular through the use of Napster. It helped users swap MP3 audio files. By connecting to the Napster network, you gained immediate access to tens of thousands (later, millions) of other computers and to all the MP3 files stored on those computers. Napster helped you find which computers had the songs you wanted, and then connected you directly to those computers to download the files. Other computers, in turn, would connect to your computer to download the music files you had stored on your hard disk.

Although it was still a P2P file-sharing network, Napster did use a central server to keep a catalog and index for the music files on users' computers.

Let's say, for example, you wanted to download some songs by your favorite artist. First, you simply started the Napster client software on your computer. This software accessed Napster's catalog and index servers, which you could then search. After you entered the name of your favorite artist in the Search box, Napster returned a list of users with songs by your favorite artist stored on their computers. If you were interested in downloading a particular song, you could choose a computer on the list that housed the song you wanted. Your computer would connect directly to the computer you selected and, with the click of a button, you could copy the file you wanted to your computer's hard disk.

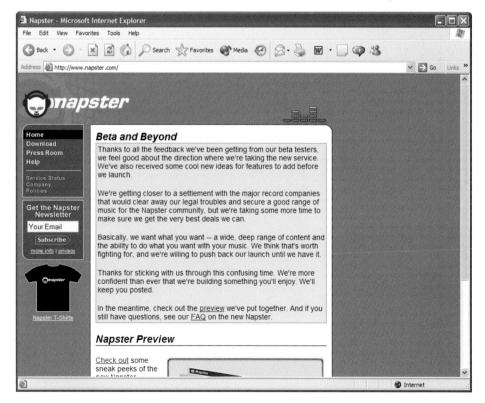

From the viewpoint of the major music studios, however, the original Napster concept enabled illegal copying of copyrighted material. In fact, because Napster used central servers to index the music files on its network, it was viewed as a party to the copyright infringement. The major record labels took Napster to court. Subsequent court rulings forced Napster to shut down its index servers—and shutting down these servers meant the Napster service wouldn't work.

More About . . . Napster

In response to the legal issues it faced, Napster reinvented itself as a more traditional subscription music service, enabling users to download copyrighted music from various labels in exchange for a monthly fee. This new Napster has retained some measure of its P2P roots, however, enabling users to swap songs that aren't copyrighted, or songs that are copyrighted but that have been licensed for sharing by the recording label, artist, or whoever controls the copyright.

Other similar file-sharing services, however, have risen in Napster's wake, without using a central index server. As a result, you still have lots of different options for swapping digital music files with other users all around the world!

More About . . . File Sharing

A key concept in a file-sharing network is that each user allows access to files on their computer's hard disk. This means you can copy files from other users' computers, and that they can copy files from yours. It's a two-way transaction. That said, every P2P file-sharing program enables you to determine what files and directories on your computer other users can see and copy. After all, you wouldn't want anyone on the Internet with the same P2P software to look at and copy any file they want on your computer, such as confidential job-related information or your personal diary. To protect your system from this type of file theft, all these programs block other users from changing any files on your computer, viewing documents you want kept private, or copying files you don't want copied.

 To gain more information about sharing music with friends and family, go to the CD-ROM segment *Digital Music: Sharing.*

P2P File-Sharing Services

Although the legality of P2P file sharing is still under debate, it remains a popular way for users to find songs they can't find on more traditional file-download sites. Napster is probably the best-known P2P file-sharing service, but there are other services that attract more users today. The next few sections provide a quick look at the services with the most users and the most songs available for swapping:

✦ Audiogalaxy

✦ Gnutella

✦ KaZaA

✦ MusicCity Morpheus

 Because the Internet is a constantly evolving environment, some of the sites we discuss in the following section may change. To find out where you can get up-to-date information, see the table at the end of this chapter.

Audiogalaxy

The Audiogalaxy P2P file-sharing service uses a Web-based interface. To use Audiogalaxy, however, you must first download and install the Audiogalaxy Satellite software. This software runs in the background and keeps your computer connected to the Audiogalaxy network while you access the Audiogalaxy site using a Web browser. You perform all your search and downloading functions from the Audiogalaxy Web site. Because Audiogalaxy uses a familiar Web-based interface, it's one of the easiest to use P2P services on the Internet.

This service stores some files directly on Audiogalaxy's servers, whereas others are available for downloading from other Audiogalaxy users' computers. Although it blocks access to some copyrighted material, it still offers an impressive amount of music for downloading.

Gnutella

Unlike Napster, which relied on a central index server to enable users to share files, Gnutella uses a totally decentralized network and technology. Instead of connecting to a central index server, users that connect to the Gnutella network link directly to the computer of another user who's currently on the network. Each computer on the network connects to several other computers, maintaining a list of its own songs as well as songs on the other computers to which it's connected.

6

You connect to the Gnutella network using any one of several Gnutella *client* software programs, including the most popular ones, BearShare and LimeWire. You can download these or other clients from the Gnutelliums Web site. To use Gnutella, you start the network's client software on your computer. It looks for other computers on the Internet running similar software to connect to. Once you're connected, you can search the Gnutella network for the songs you want. The client searches any computers you're connected to, and they pass on the search to the computers they're connected to, and so on, until the song you're searching for is located. You can then use the Gnutella client to copy that file from its host computer to yours.

KaZaA

KaZaA uses FastTrack technology, which is similar to the technology behind Gnutella and Napster. Like Gnutella, FastTrack doesn't use central servers. Instead, KaZaA performs all searching and downloading directly from one peer PC to another.

There are three ways to access the KaZaA network: the KaZaA Media Desktop software, the KaZaA Winamp plug-in, or the KaZaA Web site. You can download the software and Winamp plug-in directly from the KaZaA Web site. In fact, users have downloaded several million copies of the KaZaA software, making it one of the most popular P2P file-sharing programs.

MusicCity Morpheus

MusicCity's Morpheus file-sharing network used to use the same technology as KaZaA, but now connects to the Gnutella network. It works like other Gnutella clients, but features an interface that's easier to use. You use the Morpheus software to search the Gnutella network for the files you want, and download them directly to your computer.

 To visit some of the P2P file-sharing services we've found on the Web, see the table at the end of this chapter.

Keeping Your System Secure

Whether you prefer digital audio archives, subscription music services, or peer-to-peer sharing services, downloading music can be a lot of fun. It can also, however, pose some security hazards to your computer system. Specifically, if your computer is configured improperly, other users could gain access to confidential information on your hard drive. In addition, downloading files over the Internet can put you at greater risk of infecting your system with a virus. Finally, in the course of installing the software you need to download or share music, you may inadvertently download *spyware* or *adware* to your system. These programs occasionally display advertisements or upload information about your surfing habits to a central server without your knowledge.

Trading Files Safely

The whole idea behind P2P file-sharing systems is to swap files. That means you copy files from other users' computers, and they copy files from yours. This concerns some users, who don't want other users poking around their computer's hard disks.

In reality, there isn't much to worry about. All the major file-sharing services use software that limits file sharing only to those files and folders that you designate. It does this by creating a folder on your hard drive in which you store the items you want to share. (The name of this folder differs from program to program; check your program's help system for more information.) Anything in this folder is up for grabs; anything outside it remains private. Of course, you have to make sure you put only the files and folders you want to share in this folder.

Other users can access your computer only when you're connected to a file-sharing network. You can sever all contact by using the file-sharing software to log off from the service, and then shut down the software. When you're not logged on to the network, no other users can even connect to your computer, let alone copy files from it.

6

Protecting Your System from Viruses

Anytime you download a file from the Internet, you risk infecting your computer with a computer virus. Computer *viruses* are nasty rogue programs that can change or delete files on your hard disk or even cause your entire computer system to crash. To avoid infecting your system, you'll need to take a few precautions.

What Not to Download

It's technically impossible for a music file to infect your system with a computer virus. What is possible, however, is for you to inadvertently download another file type that can contain a computer virus. For this reason, you must be absolutely certain when downloading digital music that the file you're downloading is, in fact, a digital audio file. You can tell by checking the file's *extension*—that is, the three letters appended to the end of the file's name. For example, files whose names end in ".mp3" are MP3 files. Likewise, files whose names end in ".wma" are WMA files. (You learned about the various audio file formats in Chapter 5.)

You especially want to be careful when downloading files that are executable programs— typically, files with .exe, .pif, .bat, or .vbs extensions. When launched, these types of files, unlike music files, can infect your computer with a computer virus. It's sometime necessary to download and install these types of files; however, these extensions are not music file formats. Therefore, if you think you're downloading a song and it has one of these extensions, simply delete it from your hard disk.

 Don't be tricked by users adding a fake .mp3 file extension to EXE files, like this: *myfile.mp3.exe*. The expectation is that you won't notice the .exe extension, and will think you've downloaded a regular MP3 file. When you try to play the file, you instead launch a program, which typically contains a virus. You should always take caution when downloading any file from the Internet. Always make sure your anti-virus software has scanned a file before you open it.

Use Anti-Virus Software

The best way to protect your system against unwanted viruses is to use an *anti-virus* software program. Anti-virus programs continually scan your system for any sign of

infection. They also scan each file you download to make sure it's clean. The two most poplar anti-virus programs are The Norton AntiVirus® (shown here) and McAfee VirusScan®. Both do a good job scanning for infecting files and disinfecting or deleting any infected files they find.

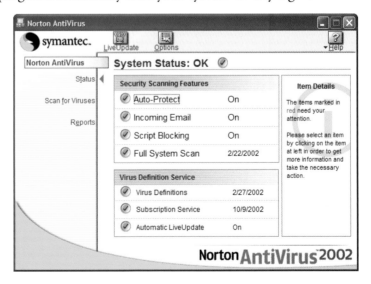

Avoiding Spyware

Although spyware, also called adware, is not a virus, it is, in most cases, a program that is downloaded to your system inadvertently when you download certain file-sharing services. These programs compromise your privacy, lurking in the background whenever you're connected to the P2P network, occasionally popping up advertisements, and, more insidiously, tracking your surfing habits. For example, spyware tracks the URLs visited by the user and sent that data to the host computer—without the user's knowledge or consent.

You can avoid installing spyware on your system by carefully watching your screen when you install file-sharing programs on your computer. Most installation routines ask you whether you want to install these additional programs (although they may disguise their true nature); simply choose not to install any program other than the main file-sharing program.

Go to the CD-ROM and select the segment:

✦ *Music Files: Downloading* to learn more about the steps and issues in downloading music from the Internet.

✦ *Media Libraries* to learn about music libraries and their uses.

✦ *Internet Radio* to gain an understanding of the benefits and uses of Internet Radio.

✦ *Digital Music: Sharing* to gain more information about sharing music with friends and family.

Go online to **www.LearnwithGateway.com** and log on to select:

✦ *Internet Links and Resources*
  ✦ *Internet Record Labels and Artist Resources*
  ✦ *Online Music Stores*
  ✦ *Digital Music Archives and Search Engines*
  ✦ *Digital Subscription Music Services*
  ✦ *Internet Radio and Streaming Audio*
  ✦ *Music Management Software*
  ✦ *Online Music Databases*
  ✦ *P2P File-Sharing Services*
✦ *FAQs*

With the *Survive & Thrive* series, refer to *Use and Care for Your PC* for more information on:

✦ *Saving and organizing files*

Refer to *Communicate and Connect to the Internet* for more information on:

✦ *Adding Web sites to your favorites list*

Gateway offers a hands-on training course that covers many of the topics in this chapter. Additional fees may apply. Call **888-852-4821** for enrollment information. If applicable, please have your customer ID and order number ready when you call.

CHAPTER 7

Recording Your Own CDs

132 Understanding CD Formats and Media
Discover the different types of CDs

137 Choosing CD-Recording Software
Find the right CD-burner software

139 Recording a CD
Copy digital music files from your computer to a CD

168 Creating CD Labels and Jewel Case Inserts
Make professional looking CD labels and inserts

You've finally done it. After hours of downloading songs from the Internet and copying tracks from your own CDs, you've built the ideal music collection, incorporating music and artists of every genre. You've organized your music files and built playlists that would make even the most seasoned DJ weep. There's only one problem: the only way you've managed to enjoy this dazzling array of music is by parking yourself in front of the computer.

Fortunately, you can easily transfer music files on your computer to a CD (a process called *burning*), which can then be played on any standard CD player. This means you can enjoy your vast music collection using your home stereo system, your car stereo, or your portable CD player. As an added bonus, you can even copy your vinyl-record and cassette-tape collection to CDs. To add polish to your music projects, you can create your own CD labels and inserts, which may contain a list of the song titles and artists on your CD.

If your system has a recordable CD drive and runs Windows XP, you already have the software you need to record your own CDs. Likewise, you probably have the software you need even if your system doesn't run Windows XP but has a CD-RW drive installed. If not, there are plenty of affordable CD-burning programs to choose from. You'll learn about them in this chapter.

Understanding CD Formats and Media

Before you get to the nuts and bolts of recording your own CDs, it's a good idea to gain a basic understanding of how CD recording works—that is, how a CD actually stores information on its surface. You'll also benefit from a solid knowledge of the various CD formats available to you.

When a commercial audio CD is created, the CD's manufacturer stamps a disc to create *pits* on the surface. Smooth (non-pitted) areas of the disc are called *lands*. A tiny laser beam in your CD player or your computer's CD drive "reads" these pits, translating them into the digital bits and bytes that make up a piece of music (for an audio CD) or computer file (for a data CD).

CD burners work in a similar way, except that instead of stamping the pits and lands that contain music data into the CD, they use a high-powered laser to blast away the underside of specially treated discs to create the equivalent of pits and lands. Instead of drilling a pit into the disc, however, the laser heats a dye that absorbs light at a specific frequency. This dulls the surface of the disc, creating the equivalent of a pit. A less intense laser in your CD player or CD drive can then read data from the disc without marking its surface.

Although you can't re-record over the pits on a commercial audio CD, you can burn new pits onto special blank CDs using the laser built into your computer's recordable CD drive (CD burner). Blank compact discs come in two different formats: CD-R (compact disc-recordable) and CD-RW (compact disc-rewritable).

You learned in Chapter 4 that you can record to CD-RW discs only by using a CD-RW drive. CD-R discs, however, can be recorded using either type of drive. For more information about recordable disc drives, refer to Chapter 4.

CD-R

Any time you create an audio CD, you use CD-R format blank discs. That's because nearly all CD players and CD drives can read this format. CD-R is the most common type of blank compact disc. CD-R discs are "write once, read many," because you can record music on a single disc only once, but you can play the disc as many times as you want. Once a CD-R has been written to (that is, once you've recorded music or some other type of data on it), it becomes a CD-ROM. The ROM in CD-ROM stands for read-only memory, meaning that unlike a CD-R, which can be read and written to, you can only read from a CD-ROM.

Once you've recorded music (or data) onto a CD-R, it's done; you can't go back and re-record over it. If you don't like what you recorded or if an error occurred, simply throw the disc away and burn a new one.

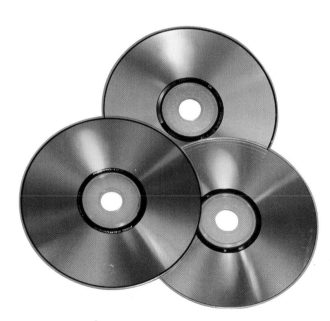

There are two different kinds of blank CD-R discs: one for audio recording and one for general data recording. If you're recording an audio CD, you might want to use a blank CD-R that is designated for audio recording; these discs cost a bit more than plain data CD-Rs because they're a little higher quality and a portion of the price goes into a royalty fund for musicians and record labels. Both types of CD-Rs, however, can be used to record audio CDs.

7

If you plan to record a CD using a home CD recorder (that is, one connected to your home stereo rather than on your computer), you must use the special audio CD-Rs. General-purpose CD-Rs will not work.

If you were to peel apart a CD-R disc, be it a general-purpose disc or one designated for use in audio recording, you'd find that it contains five layers of material. As shown in Figure 7-1, the top layer of a CD-R disc (below the optional paper label) consists of a scratch-resistant or printable coating. Next is a layer of lacquer, followed by a reflective layer, colored either gold or silver. The next layer is the important recording layer, where the recording laser burns its tiny pits. Finally, a clear plastic composes the bottom layer. The composition of these layers makes the CD-R format different from the rewritable CD-RW format, discussed in the next section.

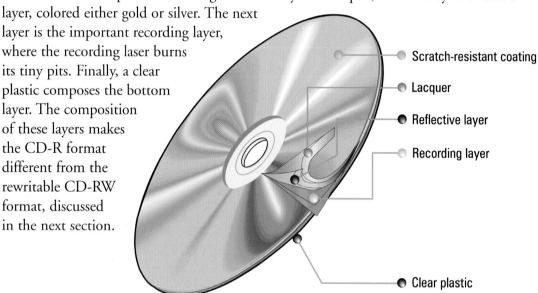

Figure 7-1 CD-R disc layers.

CD-RW

If you want to add data to a CD over a period of days or even weeks, or if you want to record over previously recorded material, you want a rewritable CD, *CD-RW*. Rewritable CDs, which cost more than CD-Rs, let you write over existing data over and over. In other words, it's a "write many, read many" format. CD-RW discs are most useful for recording text data as opposed to audio because many audio CD and players also can't read CD-RW discs. For these reasons (and the added expense of buying blank discs), you shouldn't use the CD-RW format for recording audio CDs.

 CD-RWs are also better for text data because they provide an easy way to frequently update data on the CD.

A CD-RW disc contains seven distinct layers—two more than a CD-R disc. As shown in Figure 7-2, the top layer (below the optional paper label) is the scratch-resistant or printable coating, followed by the lacquer and reflective layers. The fourth layer, however, is a dielectric layer, followed by the recording layer, followed by another dielectric layer. The way the actual recording happens is that the dye in the recording layer is heated to a non-reflective state, thus producing the simulated pits. Then to add new data, the laser reheats the dye to make it translucent. The dye is then reheated again to simulate the pits that correspond to the new data. The upper and lower dielectric layers "sandwich" the recording layer, protecting it from overheating during the heating and reheating process. Clear plastic composes the very bottom layer.

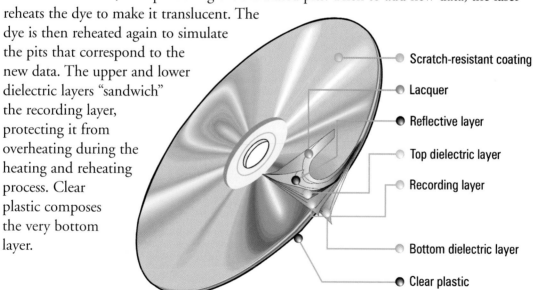

Figure 7-2 CD-RW disc layers.

Because many CDs—not to mention DVDs—are exactly the same size and color, you might not be able to identify a disc's media type simply by looking at it. If the media type is not printed on the disc itself, look at the original packaging to determine whether the disc is a CD-ROM, CD-R, or CD-RW—or if it's a DVD disc of some sort.

More About . . . CD Standards

To ensure that you can record a CD on one system and play it on another, the compact-disc industry has established standards for recording audio and other types of data on CD. The standards are for how the data is recorded (i.e., commercial discs or software), not for blank discs.

✦ Audio standards. The standard for recording audio data is the Red Book standard. According to the Red Book standard, audio CDs can hold up to 74 minutes of music, plus a table of contents for the disc's tracks. Newer recordable audio CDs, however, can hold up 80 minutes of music; these blank CDs are for audio recording only, and can't be used to store data.

✦ Data standards. The standards for recording computer data are the Yellow Book and Orange Book standards. According to these standards, CD-R and CD-RW discs can hold up to 650 MB of information.

Taking Care of Your CDs

Everything you do to care for your normal audio CDs—and a little more—applies to CD-R and CD-RW. That's because recordable and rewritable CDs are more susceptible to sunlight, heat, and humidity than normal CDs. CD-Rs and CD-RWs are more vulnerable because the disc's recording layer has to be sensitive enough for a CD burner's low-powered laser to burn it. To ensure long disc life, avoid scratching the disc surface or spilling liquids on the disc. Also avoid leaving the CD in direct sunlight or hot cars. In addition, you can write on or label the top of the disc, but don't write or put labels on the bottom side because that's the music side. Finally, always put your CD in a *jewel case*, a plastic case with a special tray for holding the CD, or sleeve when it's not being used.

When you buy an audio CD at the store, it often comes in its own jewel case, which contains an insert containing the CD's cover art and album information such as song lists, lyrics, and the like. You can also buy empty jewel cases for recordable CDs. In some cases, these cases come with the CDs themselves; otherwise, they can be bought separately. (Note that CD-Rs and CD-RWs sold without jewel cases, usually packaged on a spindle instead, are significantly less expensive.)

Choosing CD-Recording Software

Before you fire up your computer recording studio, you should know that standard audio CD players and computers differ in how they store and play audio clips. As mentioned in the preceding section, most audio CDs store clips in the CDA format. Computers, on the other hand, store audio clips in various formats, including MP3 and WMA.

For this reason, to record CDs, your computer must have special CD-recording software that can convert the files stored on your computer into a format that standard CD players can read. In addition, this software organizes the songs you want to record and burns those songs onto a blank CD-R disc.

Many digital music players offer CD-burning features. Depending on what type of player is installed on your machine, it may do the trick. If not, or if you want to use a more full-featured program, there are several free-standing CD-recording programs on the market.

Because opinions vary on which CD-recording program is the best, try downloading a shareware version of a program and using it for a while before purchasing the full version. However, first check your own computer to see if the manufacturer installed a CD-recording program.

Digital music players that you use to burn your own CDs include:

+ Windows Media Player

+ MusicMatch Jukebox

+ Liquid Player

+ RealOne Player

 Later in this chapter, you'll learn how to burn CDs using Windows Media Player and MusicMatch Jukebox. Because the Windows XP operating system includes Windows Media Player, it's a popular choice for burning audio CDs.

As mentioned, free-standing CD-recording programs may be more full-featured than the CD-recording software found with digital music players. For example, in addition to enabling users to burn CDs, many free-standing programs include the functionality to create CD labels and jewel case inserts.

7

Popular free-standing CD-recording programs include:

✦ **Easy CD Creator®.** This program by Roxio™ is a popular choice, because it's often preinstalled on new computers. Easy CD Creator can not only be used to record CDs, but it can also be used to copy songs from other CDs directly to your new audio CD and combine digital audio files and tracks from CDs in the same new CD.

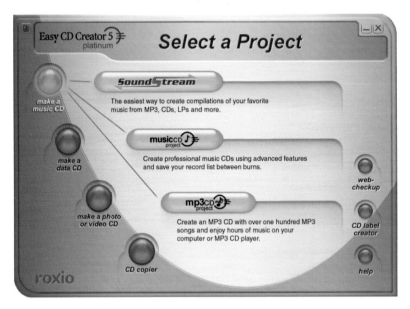

 To explore the key features of Roxio Easy CD Creator, go to the Web segment *Easy CD Creator Overview* within the Roxio lesson.

✦ **Click 'N Burn™ Pro.** This program offers the basic tools for duplicating CDs, backing up data, and creating custom audio CDs, as well as a full complement of features that appeal to high-end users. If you're a musician, for example, and need to make multiple copies of CDs for distribution, you'll appreciate Click 'N Burn's ability to support as many as four CD burners. Click 'N Burn also uses BurnProof technology, giving you more trouble-free recordings.

✦ **MP3 CD Maker.** This program enables direct MP3-to-CD burning, with no interim WAV files involved. It also includes automatic volume normalization (so that songs recorded at different volumes will play back at a similar volume) and the ability to print CD covers.

✦ **Nero.** In addition to burning audio CDs, this program also supports DVD recording and both track-at-once and disc-at-once recording (explained later in the chapter). It supports all major models of CD-R and CD-RW drives.

To explore the key features of Nero Burning ROM, go to the Web segment *Nero Overview* within the Nero lesson.

If you decide to purchase CD-recording software instead of using software that's already installed on your system, you'll need to install it yourself. (In some cases, you may need to download the software from the Internet first.) You learned how to download and install a digital music player in Chapter 5. The process for downloading and installing CD-recording software is similar.

 To learn about the features of popular CD burning software, go to the CD-ROM segment *CD Burning Software*.

Recording a CD

Once CD-recording software is installed on your computer, you're ready to begin burning your own CDs. Before you do, however, you'll need to decide what type of CD you want to burn:

+ A CD that can be played in any audio CD player

+ A CD that can be played by an MP3 CD player

This section has step-by-step instructions for recording both types of CDs, as well as information about recording an entire CD already in your collection. You'll even learn how to record music from albums and cassette tapes that you have in your "pre-digital" music library, including cleaning up the notorious pops and clicks on old vinyl records and the hiss from audio tape when you record it on new CDs. Before you begin recording, however, you should take a few steps to prepare your system and configure your recording options. This will be covered next.

Preparing Your System for Recording

Copying large audio files from your hard drive to a blank CD-R requires tremendous processing power. For this reason, you should exit all other open programs, including your e-mail software, Web browser, even your system's screen saver and programs running in the background, to ensure that they don't consume processing power better used by your recording program. Otherwise, the recording process may be interrupted by activity in one of these programs. If the recording process is interrupted in any way, the file you're recording might be damaged—or the recording process itself might be halted and an error message displayed.

7

Configuring Recording Method

Depending on what type of CD-recording program you use, you may be able to configure various recording methods to suit the type of recording you want to make. For example, you may be able to configure any of the following settings:

◆ **Multi-session CDs.** A multi-session CD includes both audio and computer data. You might use this option if you're mixing normal CD audio with MP3 or WMA files, which are considered computer data. If you're recording a straight audio CD, you can bypass this option. If you select this option, you'll only be able to play the CD in a computer CD player, because most home CD players do not support multi-session.

◆ **Track-by-track recording.** When you record track-by-track, the CD burner turns off its laser between tracks, and uses this time to read the data for the next track. This places a standard two-second blank space between each song on your CD. Most CD-recorder programs record in track-by-track mode by default because it typically produces fewer errors than recording the entire disc at once, discussed next. In most cases, you'll want to select this option for creating audio CDs that can be played on any CD player.

◆ **Entire-disc recording.** If you want to eliminate the two-second gap between songs, you can opt to record the entire disc at once. This option combines all the songs into one giant file, so that the laser doesn't have to be turned off between tracks. Because the entire-disc recording process involves copying such a large file, it can result in more recording errors than track-by-track recording. For most users, track-by-track recording is the better choice. Not all CD players can play a CD burned using entire-disc recording. Easy CD Creator calls entire-disc recording the Disc-at-Once mode; you can select it from Easy CD Creator's Record CD Setup dialog box.

◆ **Test recording.** Most CD-recorder programs give you the option to create a "test write" before the actual CD-recording process begins. This test steps you through the entire burning process, but with the recording laser turned off.

 You should opt for a test write the first few times you make CDs to get the hang of it or if you think there might be some problems with the recording process. Otherwise, skip the test (which takes exactly as long as the real recording) and go right to the burning.

Recording an Audio CD

As mentioned previously, you can use your computer to burn two types of CDs: those playable by any standard CD player, and those playable by MP3 players. In this section, you'll learn how to create the former using Windows Media Player, MusicMatch Jukebox, and Easy CD Creator.

When you create a CD playable by any standard CD player, your CD-recording software converts the MP3, WMA, and other similar music files on your computer to adhere to the CDA format used by standard audio CDs. Although the specific instructions for recording a CD differ from program to program, the general process follows these steps (see Figure 7-3):

1. Using a playlist, you assemble and organize the digital music files you want to burn to a CD.
2. The software converts the files (typically in MP3 or WMA format) to WAV-format files.
3. The software copies the WAV-format files to CDA-format files on the CD-R disc.
4. The software "closes" the CD so no other files can be recorded on it.

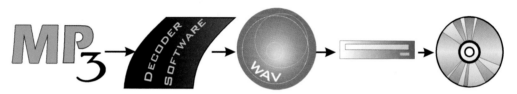

Figure 7-3 The process of recording an audio CD from MP3 files.

 To learn how to convert or rip a music track to a CD using the Roxio Easy CD Creator, go to the Web segment *Track: Ripping* within the Roxio lesson.

To learn how to rip a musical track using Nero Burning ROM, go to the Web segment *Track: Ripping* within the Nero lesson.

Using Windows Media Player to Burn an Audio CD

To burn an audio CD using Windows Media Player on Windows XP, first start Windows Media Player by clicking the start button, choosing All Programs, and choosing Windows Media Player. Alternatively, if there's a shortcut to Windows Media Player on your desktop, double-click it to start the program. Then, do the following:

1. In the Windows Media Player window, click the Media Library button in the command bar on the left side of the program window.
2. Click the New Playlist button, located near the top of the Windows Media Player window.
3. Using the steps outlined in Chapter 5, add the tracks you want to record to the playlist.

7

④ Select the playlist, and then organize the tracks in the playlist so they appear in the order you want them recorded on the CD. To do so, drag tracks up or down the list and drop them where you want them.

 As you add songs to the playlist for your CD, note the total time for the playlist in the lower-right corner, below the song list. This time must not exceed 74 minutes; otherwise, the playlist won't fit on a standard CD-R disc. In fact, it's a good idea to keep the total time a minute or two shorter than that to leave time for spaces between songs.

⑤ In the Windows Media Player window, click the Copy to CD or Device button in the command bar on the left side of the program window.

6 In the Music to Copy list, select the tracks from the playlist that you want to copy. Windows Media Player assumes you want to record all the tracks in the list to a blank CD. To prevent Windows Media Player from copying a particular track in the list, clear the check box next to the track to deselect it.

Status

Minutes free

7 Insert a blank CD-R disc in your computer's CD-recorder drive.

8 If your recordable CD drive is not already selected in the Music On Device list (in the right-hand pane), click it to select it.

9 Click the Copy Music button in the upper-right corner of the window. Windows Media Player converts each track to WAV format, then to CDA format, and then copies them to your blank CD-R disc.

Progress bar

Progress bar

 This operation can take several minutes, depending on the length of the selected tracks, the speed of your computer, and the transfer rate of your CD burner.

10 When Windows Media Player finishes the burning process, it displays a Closing disc message, a Complete message, and then displays the contents of the CD in the Music on Device pane.

 If you try to copy too much music to the CD-R disc, Windows Media Player displays a "May Not Fit" message, instead. If you see this message, you'll need to rethink your playlist and burn another disc.

 You'll notice that the Music to Copy section Status column now reads Will not fit. That's because you probably just filled your CD.

Using MusicMatch Jukebox to Burn an Audio CD

MusicMatch Jukebox includes a utility called Burner Plus, which you can use to burn a CD from your favorite MP3, WMA, or WAV files. To record an audio CD using Burner Plus, first start MusicMatch Jukebox by choosing the start button, choosing All Programs, MusicMatch, and MusicMatch Jukebox. Alternatively, if there's a shortcut to MusicMatch Jukebox on your desktop, double-click it to start the program. Then, do the following:

1. Insert a blank CD-R disc in your computer's CD-recorder drive.
2. In the Music Library window, create or select the playlist you want to burn to CD.

 To create a playlist in MusicMatch, you simply click the My Library button and double-click the track or click and drag it to add it to the playlist.

3. Click Burn.

 To learn how to create music CDs from your playlist using MusicMatch, go to the Web segment *Music CDs: Creating* within the MusicMatch Jukebox lesson.

I like the Movies by Bernie Clarke — 3:56
I saw Jesus Yesterday by Bernie Clarke — 2:29
Bernie Clarke - If You Knew by Bernie Clarke — 1:28
My Brother From Buffalo by Bernie Clarke — 3:30
No Rapido by Bernie Clarke — 3:43
Prettier by Bernie Clarke — 3:33
Seeing Him Again by Bernie Clarke — 3:16
Stressed Out Heart by Bernie Clarke — 4:49
The Beach by Bernie Clarke — 3:29
Fool's Gold by Bernie Clarke — 5:37

Disc_040102_1

49 % (35:55 of 73:20)

④ The Burner Plus window opens. To organize the tracks in the playlist so they appear in the order you want them recorded on the CD, drag tracks up or down the list and drop them where you want them.

⑤ Click the Burn button. Burner Plus converts each track to WAV format, then to CDA format, and then copies them to your blank CD-R disc. As the songs are burned to the disc, you'll see a status box and when the burning is complete, the status box will read Finishing disc until everything is 100 percent complete.

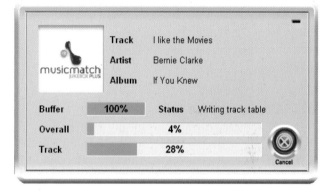

Track — I like the Movies
Artist — Bernie Clarke
Album — If You Knew
Buffer — 100%
Status — Writing track table
Overall — 4%
Track — 28%
Cancel

This operation can take several minutes, depending on the length of the selected tracks, the speed of your computer, and the transfer rate of your CD burner.

⑥ Click the Return to Burner Plus button, and then click the Close button on the Burner Plus window to return to MusicMatch Jukebox.

Burn Successful
Return to Burner Plus

Buffer — 100%
Status — Disc finished
Overall — 100%
Track — 100%

7

Using Easy CD Creator to Burn an Audio CD

Burning an audio CD with free-standing CD-recording software such as Roxio's Easy CD Creator is easy and intuitive. To burn CDs using Roxio, you use the Project Selector. Follow these steps:

1. On a Windows XP machine, start Easy CD Creator by clicking the start button, choosing All Programs, Roxio Easy CD Creator, and then choosing Project Selector.
2. In the Easy CD Creator Project Selector, select Make a Music CD, and then click Music CD Project.

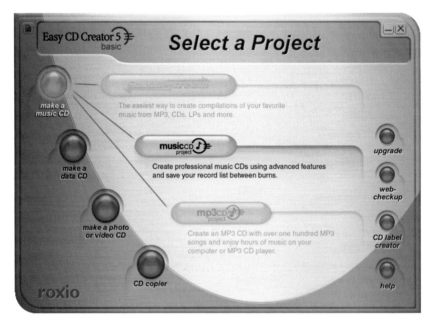

 To practice recording music to a CD using the Roxio Easy CD Creator, go to the Web segment *Music: Recording* within the Roxio lesson.

③ A new CD Project window opens. Insert a blank CD-R disc into your computer's CD recorder drive.

④ In the **Select Source Files** list, navigate to the folder that contains the music files you want to copy to CD.

⑤ A list of files in the selected folder appears in the Source window. Press and hold down the **CTRL** key on your keyboard as you click the files you want to copy.

 Put your mouse pointer over the selected files and a box will appear that shows you the properties of your selected files, including the duration and size.

⑥ When all the desired files are selected, click **Add**.

 If you like, type a title for the CD in the New CD Title text box and a description of the CD or a list of artists in the Artist Name text box (located in the Record panel on the left).

⑦ The selected files are displayed in the Audio CD Layout Window. To organize the tracks so they appear in the order you want them recorded on the CD, drag tracks up or down the list and drop them where you want them.

7

As you add songs to the list for your CD, note the total time for the CD at the bottom of the window, below the song list. This time must not exceed 74 minutes; otherwise, the songs won't fit on a standard CD-R disc. In fact, it's a good idea to keep the total time a minute or two shorter than that to leave time for spaces between songs.

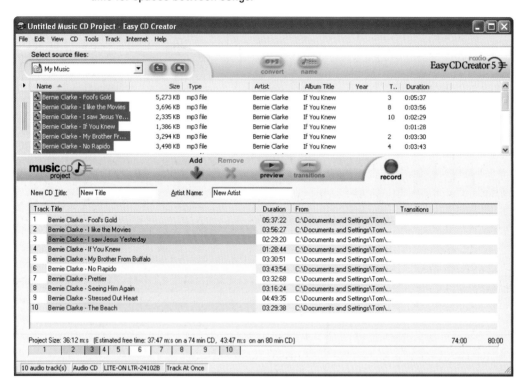

8 Click **Record**. The Record CD Setup dialog box opens.

At this point you can change the recording method, by clicking Options, and then selecting the option of your choice.

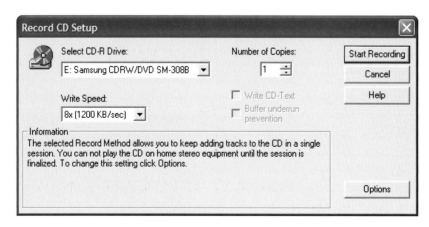

9 Click the **Start Recording** button.

⑩ The Record CD Progress dialog box opens showing you the process of the CD burn.

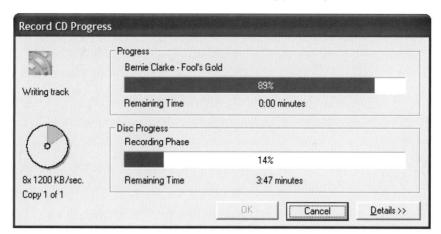

⑪ The Record Complete dialog box opens. Click **Finalize** if you're done recording your CD.

 If you don't click Finalize, you can add tracks to this CD later; however, you cannot play the CD on home stereo equipment until the session is finalized. Likewise, once the CD is finalized, you cannot add additional tracks to the CD.

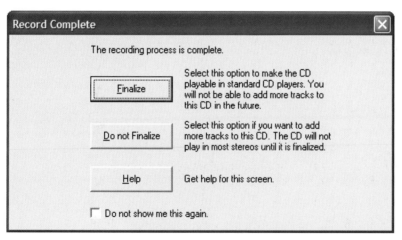

⑫ The Closing CD progress bar appears and when the CD's closed, you'll see the CD created successfully message. Click **OK** and you're done.

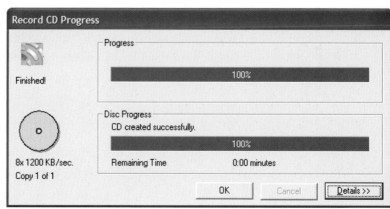

7

If a Save CD Project changes dialog opens, click No unless you really want to save the CD layout to your hard disk as well.

> ### More About . . . Burning Audio CDs
>
> You can also use Easy CD Creator to copy songs from other CDs directly to your new audio CD. Just insert the CD with the songs to copy into your CD-ROM drive, pull down the Select Source Files list, choose your CD-ROM drive, and then choose the track(s) you want to copy. This adds the selected song(s) to your new music project. You can also combine digital audio files and tracks from CDs on the same CD; Easy CD Creator will prompt you when to insert and remove the audio CD and the blank CD.

 To practice recording music to a CD using Nero Burning ROM, go to the Web segment *Music CD: Burning* within the Nero lesson.

Recording an MP3 CD

When you record an audio CD, you're limited to either 74 or 80 minutes of music, depending on the type of blank CD-R you use. However, you can fit more music on a CD if you leave the songs in their compressed format. In fact, a disc full of MP3 files can house upwards of 200 individual songs! The downside? You won't be able to play your MP3 CD in most audio CD players. Unless you have a special player capable of reading MP3 files, you'll be limited to playing the disc in your computer's CD-ROM drive.

A so-called "MP3 CD" isn't limited to only MP3 files. You can also create this type of data CD with WMA-format audio files—assuming your playback devices support the WMA format.

Unlike burning an audio CD, which requires the CD-recording software to convert files from MP3 to WMA and then to CDA format, no file translation is required when you burn MP3 CDs. As shown in Figure 7-4, the files go directly from your hard disk to the CD, retaining their original format. That means the recording process is faster and easier than the process for recording audio CDs.

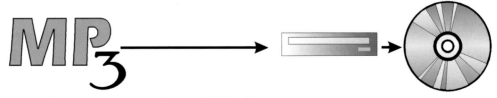

Figure 7-4 The process for recording an MP3 file CD.

In this section, you'll learn how to create your own MP3 CDs using Windows XP.

Note that the process for creating MP3 CDs using MusicMatch Jukebox and Easy CD Creator are very similar to creating regular CDs. In the MusicMatch Jukebox steps, you would click the MP3 button in step 4 rather than the Burn button. In Easy CD Creator, you click the MP3CD Project button instead.

Using Windows XP to Burn an MP3 CD

Although Windows Media Player doesn't support the creation of MP3 CDs, you can use Windows XP to copy MP3 (and WMA) files to a blank CD-R disc almost as easily as copying a standard computer file. Here's how:

1 Insert a blank CD-R disc into your CD recorder drive.

2 Click the **start** button and choose **My Computer** to open the My Computer window.

3 Navigate to and select the MP3 or WMA files you want to copy.

4 Choose **Copy the selected items** from the File and Folder Tasks section.

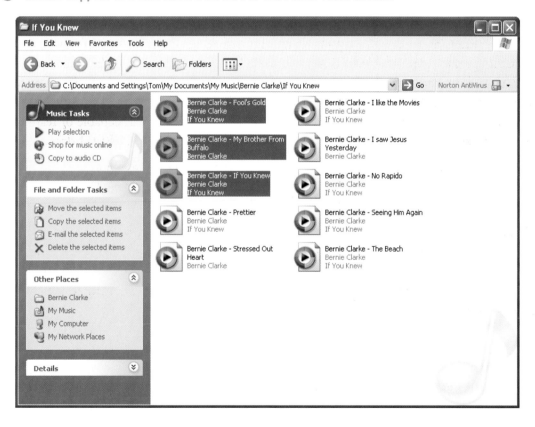

5 The Copy Items dialog box opens. Select your recordable CD drive.

6 Click **Copy**.

7 Windows copies the selected files to a temporary folder, viewable when you return to My Computer and select your recordable CD drive. As shown here, Windows lists these files under the heading "Files Ready to Be Written to the CD." Verify that the files are correct, and then click **Write these files to CD**.

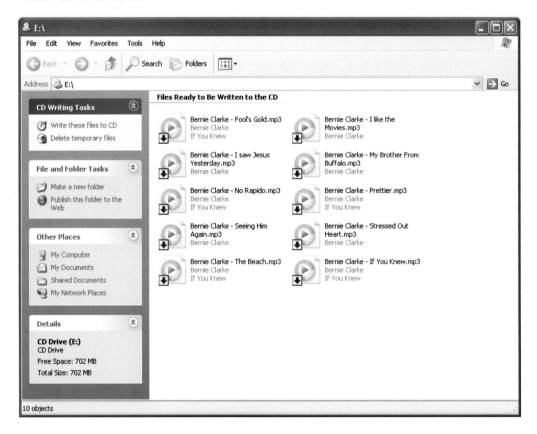

8 The CD Writing Wizard launches. Enter a name for your new CD, and then click Next.

9 The wizard asks you if you want to make an audio CD or a data CD. Select the Make a Data CD option then click Next.

10 The wizard now writes the selected files to your blank CD-R disc, displaying a progress bar during the process. When the process is finished, the wizard ejects the newly written CD and displays a message saying that you have successfully written your files to CD. Click Finish to close the wizard.

Duplicating Entire CDs

As you've just learned, it's easy to burn your own "mix" CDs. You can also use your CD-burner software to copy complete CDs, resulting in an exact digital duplicate of the original. Creating a duplicate audio CD copies the original CD to your hard disk (translating the files to WAV format), and then copies the files back (translating the files back to CD Audio format) to a new blank CD-R disc.

Not every program features a CD-duplicating function. For example, Windows Media Player doesn't duplicate CDs in this fashion. However, Easy CD Creator uses CD Copier to duplicate CDs. Follow these steps:

1 On a Windows XP machine, start Easy CD Creator by clicking the start button, choosing All Programs, Roxio Easy CD Creator, Applications, and choosing CD Copier. Alternatively, you can open the Project Selector as described earlier and choose CD copier.

2 Insert the original CD into your CD drive.

7

③ Click **CD Copier**. The CD Copier window opens

④ Select the **Source and Destination** tab.

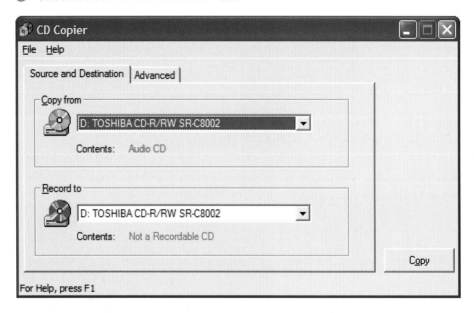

⑤ Select your CD drive in both the Copy From and Record To lists.

 If you have two CD drives, you would simply select the appropriate drives and skip step 7.

⑥ Click **Copy**. CD Copier converts the files from the original CD to WAV format and temporarily copies them to your hard disk.

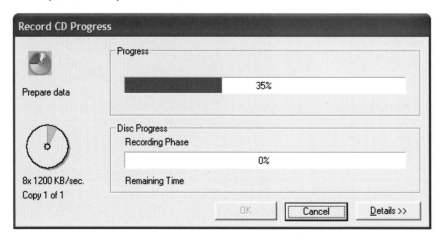

7 CD Copier prompts you to remove the original CD and insert a blank CD-R into your CD drive. Click **Retry**.

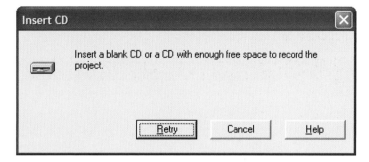

Insert CD

Insert a blank CD or a CD with enough free space to record the project.

Retry   Cancel   Help

8 Follow the on-screen instructions to finish copying the files to the new disc. The process from here is the same as steps 11-13 in the Using Easy CD Creator to Burn an Audio CD section earlier.

 To make copies of a music CD using the Roxio Easy CD Creator, go to the Web segment *CD Copier* within the Roxio lesson.

Copying LPs and Cassettes to CD

If you're a true audiophile, there's a good chance you have an extensive collection of pre-digital music—that is, vinyl records and audio cassettes. If so, you can transfer the albums in your aging collection to digital format and burn them onto CDs. (You can even convert 8-tracks if you want.) You'll get the portability, easy access, and flexibility benefits from the digital audio format—after all, it's a lot easier to listen to an audio or MP3 CD on the go than it is to lug around boxes of albums and a turntable. As an added bonus, your new digital files should last longer than aging albums and tapes.

 Because albums and cassettes are analog media, converting them to CD is a much slower process than ripping tracks from a CD. That's because you record these analog media at the same speed they play.

To make a CD copy of a vinyl record or cassette tape, you need the same equipment you use to burn a CD from any other source—namely, a computer with a sound card installed, a recordable CD drive, and CD-burner software. In addition, you'll need a few extra components connected to your computer:

✦ A turntable or cassette tape deck

✦ Audio amplifier or receiver

✦ Stereo cable

7

To connect these components to your computer, do the following:

① Connect your turntable or cassette deck to the receiver/amplifier in your home audio system.

 Although it's not recommended, you can connect a cassette deck directly to your computer. You cannot, however, connect a turntable in this fashion. Your turntable must be connected through a receiver to achieve the correct sound levels for recording.

② Run a stereo cable from the line out jacks on the receiver/amplifier's back to the line in jacks on the back of your computer.

 If you only have a single line in jack on your computer, you'll need an adapter cable that goes from separate right and left jacks to a single stereo plug.

After you've connected these components to your computer, you're almost ready to go. First, however, you need to install some special software on your computer to handle the recording process. This software converts the audio signal sent from your turntable or cassette deck to a WAV-format digital audio format. This WAV file can then be burned to a blank CD-R disc.

 You can also convert the WAV file to an MP3 or WMA file using your digital music player. These files consume less hard disk space, and can be used with portable MP3 players.

When it comes to software for converting vinyl records or cassettes to digital music files, you have several choices, including Microsoft Sound Recorder and Easy CD Creator's Spin Doctor.

 To find out where you can get information about software for converting vinyl records or cassettes to digital music files, see the table at the end of this chapter.

In addition to enabling listeners to convert their vinyl records and cassettes to digital music files, many of these software programs also enable users to remove some of the pops, crackles, and hisses from these old formats. For example, Easy CD Creator's Spin Doctor program removes pops and crackles during the recording process; in addition, you can use Easy CD Creator's SoundStream™ program to clean up files after you record them.

In the sections that follow, you'll learn how to convert the music on your vinyl records and cassettes to WAV-format digital music files using Sound Recorder and Easy CD Creator's Spin Doctor. Once you've converted these media, you can then burn them to CD just as you would any other digital music file.

 You can record all the songs on a vinyl record or cassette tape as separate files, or you can record the entire side of an LP or tape as one large file. Although you might like the convenience of recording one large file, recording separate files provides more flexibility when you burn the songs to CD or play individual songs from your music library with your digital music player.

Using Sound Recorder to Record WAV Files

To use Sound Recorder to convert songs on a vinyl record or cassette to WAV-format digital music files, follow these steps:

 Once the digital file has been created and saved, you can burn it to CD just as you would any digital audio file. (Refer to the section "Recording an Audio CD" earlier in this chapter for more detailed instructions.)

1 Click the Windows start button, point to All Programs, point to Accessories, point to Entertainment, and choose Sound Recorder. The Sound Recorder window opens.

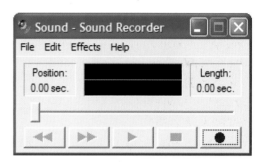

2 In the Sound Recorder window, click the File menu and choose Properties. The Properties dialog box opens.

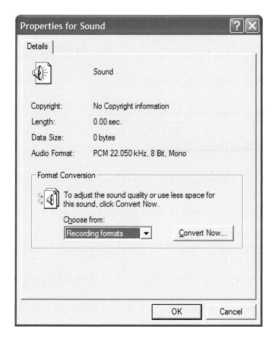

3 Open the Format Conversion list and choose Recording formats.

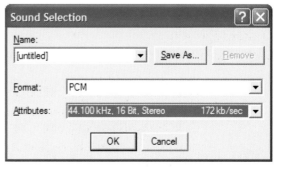

4 Click Convert Now. The Sound Selection dialog box opens.

5 Open the Name list and choose CD Quality.

6 Select the **PCM** format if it isn't already selected. (PCM stands for pulse code modulation, a particular type of digital recording.)

7 Set **Attributes** to **44.100kHz**, **16 bit, stereo, 172kb/sec**.

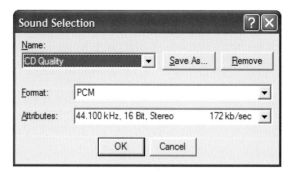

More About . . . Sound Attributes

In step 7 in the preceding exercise, you set the Attributes setting to 44.100 kHz, 16 bit, stereo, 172 kb/sec. These numbers relate to the recording speed. The first number (44.100 kHz) is the *sampling rate,* or the number of times per second the computer listens to the signal. The second value is the *resolution,* or the number of bits of data written for each sample. Reflecting the selection you made, standard audio CD playback uses a 44.1 kHz sampling rate and 16-bit resolution. This means that the system samples the signal 44,100 times per second and writes 16 bits of data for each sample.

Note, however, that CDs are actually recorded at a higher sample rate and resolution—96 kHz and 24-bit. As you might guess, the more times the software samples the signal, the more accurate the recording will be. The same holds true for the resolution. You get better sound quality from a more complete recording.

Not surprisingly, this improved quality comes at a price. Higher quality recordings result in larger files and require more resources necessary to play the file. As an example, a three-minute song recorded at 96 kHz takes just 2.15 MB, whereas the same song recorded at 320 kHz takes 7.16 MB.

8 Click **OK** to close the Sound Selection dialog box.

9 Click **OK** to close the Properties dialog box.

10 Moving to your stereo amplifier, select the correct source (phono or tape), and then cue up the record or tape you want to record at the point where you want to begin recording.

11 Back in Windows Sound Recorder, click the **Record** button.

12 From your stereo system, start playing the record or tape you want to record. Sound Recorder records the music.

13 When the music finishes, click Sound Recorder's **Stop** button.

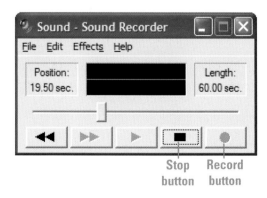

Stop button   Record button

You can choose to record the entire side of an LP or cassette as one file, or you can record each track individually. If you want to record the entire album but are recording each track individually, you'll need to repeat steps 10 through 13 for each song you want to record.

14 To save the file you just recorded, click the File menu and choose Save As.

 To lessen the pops, crackles, and hisses in your new files, you can use Easy CD Creator's SoundStream utility to clean them up before you burn them to CD. For more information, see the section "Using Easy CD Creator's SoundStream to Clean Up WAV Files and Burn a CD" later in this chapter.

When you listen to your recording, you might notice some unnecessary blank at the beginning and end of the WAV file. To trim the blank space from the beginning of the file, do the following:

1 Click the File menu and choose Open.
2 Navigate to and open the file you want to edit.
3 Move the slider to where the music begins (the flat line gets wider).
4 Click the Edit menu and choose Delete Before Current Position.

To delete blank space at the end of the file, do the following:

1 With the music file open, move the slider to where the music ends (the flat line gets narrower).
2 Click the Edit menu and choose Delete After Current Position.

Using Easy CD Creator's Spin Doctor to Record WAV Files

If you want more control over the digital copies you make of your old records or tapes, you can use the Spin Doctor program included with Easy CD Creator. (Note that this is an upgrade to the basic version.) In addition to enabling you to convert your vinyl and cassettes to digital files, Spin Doctor also helps you remove those annoying crackles, pops, and hisses in the process.

To use Spin Doctor to copy your old records and tapes, start Easy CD Creator Project Selector, and then follow these steps:

 Once the digital file has been created, you can burn it to CD just as you would any digital audio file. (Refer to the section "Recording an Audio CD" earlier in this chapter for more detailed instructions.)

7

1 Select Make a Music CD, and then click SoundStream. The SoundStream program starts.
2 Click Effects to display the effects controls.

❸ Click Spin Doctor. The Spin Doctor program starts.

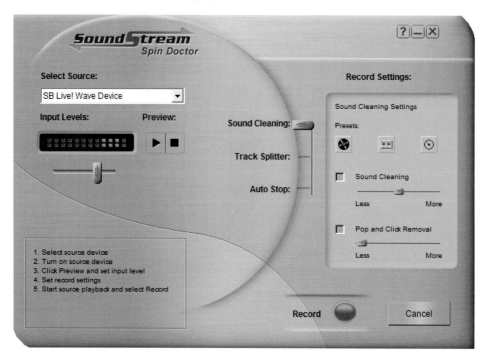

❹ Open the Select Source drop-down list and choose your sound recorder. (This is normally the sound recorder software associated with your computer's sound card.)

❺ Begin a test playback from your turntable or cassette deck, and then click Preview.

❻ Move the Input Levels slider to the right or left to adjust the recording levels; choose a level that sounds good to you.

❼ Click the Sound Cleaning option.

Presets for Tape

Presets for LP

Sound Cleaning Settings

Presets:

☐ Sound Cleaning

Less   More

☐ Pop and Click Removal

Less   More

8 If you're recording from a vinyl record, click Presets for LP. Alternatively, if you're recording from a cassette, click Presets for Tape. This automatically adjusts the Sound Cleaning and Pop and Click Removal sliders to the correct settings. (You can also adjust these sliders manually.)

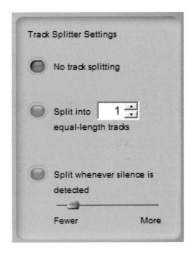

Track Splitter Settings

◉ No track splitting

◯ Split into ☐ 1 ☐ equal-length tracks

◯ Split whenever silence is detected

Fewer   More

9 Click the Track Splitter option.
10 To record an entire album side as a single file, select No track splitting. Alternatively, select Split whenever silence is detected to record a separate file for each track. If you choose the latter, use the accompanying slider to specify how much silence the program should search for.

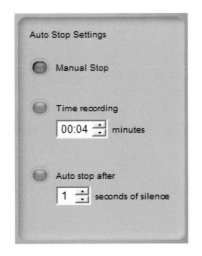

Auto Stop Settings

◉ Manual Stop

◯ Time recording
     00:04 ☐ minutes

◯ Auto stop after
     1 ☐ seconds of silence

11 Click the Auto Stop option.
12 If you want to stop the recording yourself, select Manual Stop. Alternatively, choose Auto stop after x seconds of silence if you want Spin Doctor to sense the end of an album side and stop recording automatically.

7

⑬ Click **Record**.

⑭ In the Spin Doctor dialog box, enter a name for the file.

⑮ In the Record To area, click the **File** button. (You can also record direct to CD if you wish; click the **CD** button instead.)

⑯ Click **Start Recording**.

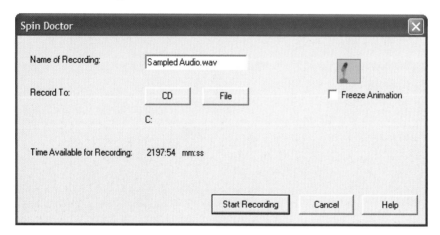

⑰ Start playing the record or tape you want to record.

⑱ Spin Doctor begins recording. If you selected the Auto Stop option, the recording stops automatically when the album side is finished playing. If not, click **Stop** when the record or tape finishes.

 Play back the recorded files to check the recording quality. If they're not to your liking, try recording the album again.

Using Easy CD Creator's SoundStream to Clean Up WAV Files and Burn a CD

If you've already recorded your WAV files (using Sound Recorder for example), you can clean up the finished product with Easy CD Creator's SoundStream application. Start Easy CD Creator Project Selector and then follow these steps:

1 Select Make a Music CD, and then click SoundStream. The SoundStream program starts.

2 Insert a blank CD-R disc into your CD recorder drive.

3 Click the Show Option Drawer button to display the program's additional utilities.

4 In the Select Source pane on the left side of the window, click Select Folder.

7

⑤ Navigate to the folder on your computer in which the WAV files you want to clean up and burn are stored.

⑥ A list of files in the selected folder appears. Press and hold down the CTRL key on your keyboard as you click the files you want to clean up and burn.

⑦ Click the Add Selected button.

⑧ In the Select Destination pane, click Select Music CD.

⑨ Select the files in the destination list, and then click Effects. The effects controls are displayed.

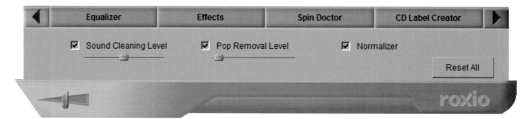

⑩ If you're cleaning a file recorded from a cassette tape, click the Sound Cleaning Level check box to select it.

⑪ Move the associated slider to the right to remove more tape hiss, or to the left to remove less tape hiss. If you move the slider too far to the right, you might decrease the high frequencies in the recording.

⑫ If you're cleaning a file recorded from a vinyl record, click the Pop Removal Level check box to select it.

⑬ Move the associated slider to the right to increase the amount of pop and click removal, or to the left to decrease the amount of pop and click removal. If you move the slider too far to the right, you might remove some of the high and low frequencies in the recording.

⑭ If you're burning tracks taken from several different sources, click the Normalizer check box to select it. *Normalizing* adjusts the volume level so all the songs play back at the same volume even if you recorded some louder or softer than others.

⑮ Click Record to burn the selected file to a blank CD-R disc.

Recording Analog Sounds

The sounds on vinyl records and cassettes aren't the only analog sounds you can record to your computer. In fact, if you have a microphone, and your sound card has a *microphone in port*, you can record just about any sound you like! You can then convert this sound to digital format using Windows Sound Recorder. To do so, first start Sound Recorder by clicking the Windows **start** button, pointing to **All Programs**, pointing to **Accessories**, pointing to **Entertainment**, and then clicking **Sound Recorder**. Then do the following:

 Once the digital file of the recorded sound has been created, you can burn it to CD just as you would any digital audio file. (Refer to the section "Recording an Audio CD" earlier in this chapter for more detailed instructions.)

1 Plug an input device such as a microphone into the input port on your sound card.

2 The buttons you use to control Sound Recorder are similar to those on VCRs or cassette recorders. To begin recording, click the **Record** button.

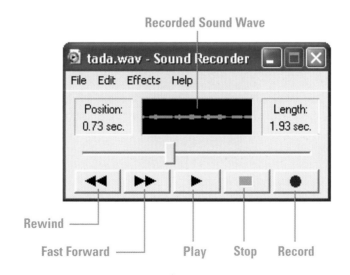

Recorded Sound Wave

Rewind

Fast Forward — Play Stop Record

③ Speak or sing into the microphone. As you record, the sound recorder window displays a graph of the incoming sound wave.

④ When you've captured the sound you want to save, click **Stop**.

⑤ To save the file, click **File**, and then choose **Save**.

⑥ Specify the folder in which you want to save the file, and type a descriptive name for the file.

⑦ Click **Save**.

 One of Sound Recorder's limitations is that it only reads and writes WAV files. If you want to save your file in a different format, you must use another software program to record it. Alternatively, you can use another program like MusicMatch Jukebox to convert the sound to another format after recording it with Sound Recorder.

Creating CD Labels and Jewel Case Inserts

Once you've burned your own CD, it's a good idea to label it so you don't confuse it with other home-made discs. Of course, you can always use a permanent marker to identify the CD, writing down the songs it contains or the artists it features. A more elegant solution, however, is to use your computer to create an artful label, and stick it on your disc.

In this section, you'll look at various software programs you can use to accomplish this. You'll also learn how to create a jewel case insert, like the ones that come with store-bought CDs, to add real polish to your music project.

Choosing Software for Labels and Inserts

You can use any of several programs to create labels and jewel case inserts for your CDs. In fact, some CD-recorder programs, including Easy CD Creator, include built-in labeling features. Free-standing CD-labeling programs, however, typically offer more options for customizing your labels and inserts. In fact, some programs even include their own labels, and devices to help you affix them to CDs.

In the sections that follow, you'll learn how to use CD Stomper® to create CD labels and jewel case inserts.

 To learn about the use and benefits of CD Labels and Jewel Inserts in the Roxio Easy CD Creator, go to the Web segment *CD Label and Jewel Insert: Creating* within the Roxio lesson.

To practice creating a CD Label and Jewel Insert using Nero Burning ROM, go to the Web segment *CD Label and Jewel Insert: Creating* within the Nero lesson.

Creating a CD Label

CD Stomper makes creating a CD label fast and easy. All you have to do is follow these steps:

1. Start the CD Stomper program by clicking the start button, All Programs, and then choosing CD Stomper, SureThing™ CD Labeler. The New dialog box opens automatically.

2. In the New dialog box, select Pro CD Labels from the SmartDesigns list.

 If, during the course of your work, you need to access the New dialog box again, click the File menu and choose New from within the SureThing CD Labeler – Stomper Edition program.

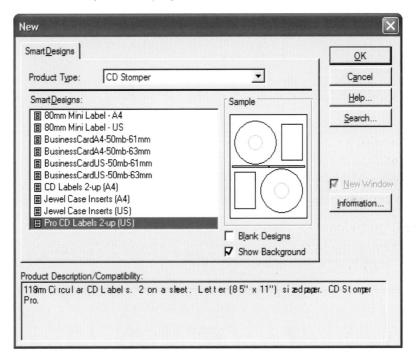

3. Click OK. A label-layout window opens.

7

④ To cycle through available designs, click the left and right arrows on the Layout bar (at the bottom of the window) and the left and right arrows on the Accent bar.

Picture tool —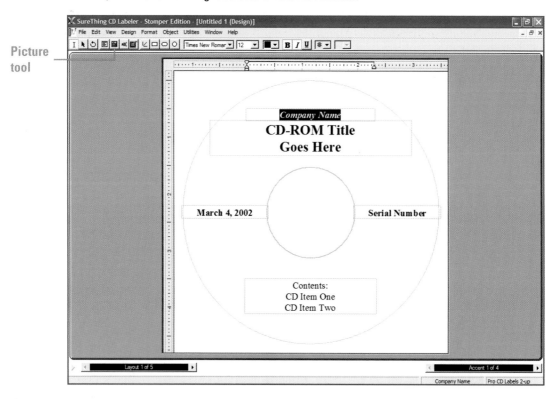

⑤ To change the formatting for any text box, select the text in the label-layout window, click the Format menu, and then select the formatting you want.

⑥ To add a picture or graphic image to your label, click the Picture Tool button (or click the Object menu, choose Tools, and choose Picture Tool).

⑦ Draw a box by left clicking and dragging where you want the image to appear.

⑧ The New Picture dialog box opens. Select the image file you want to add to the label, and click OK.

⑨ When you finish designing your label, click the File menu and choose Save As to save the label in your desired location.

⑩ To print the label, insert a blank label in your printer, click the File menu, and choose Print.

⑪ After you print the label, apply it to your new CD using the CD Stomper applicator. Make sure you center the label, and that it goes on flat, with no wrinkles.

Creating a Jewel Case Insert

To add real polish to your music project, you can create a jewel case insert, like the ones that come with store-bought CDs, for your CD's jewel case. This section demonstrates how to do this using CD Stomper.

1. Start the CD Stomper program. The New dialog box opens automatically.
2. In the New dialog box, select Jewel Case Inserts (US).
3. Click OK. The insert layout window opens.
4. To cycle through available designs, click the left and right arrows on the Layout bar (at the bottom of the window) and the left and right arrows on the Accent bar.

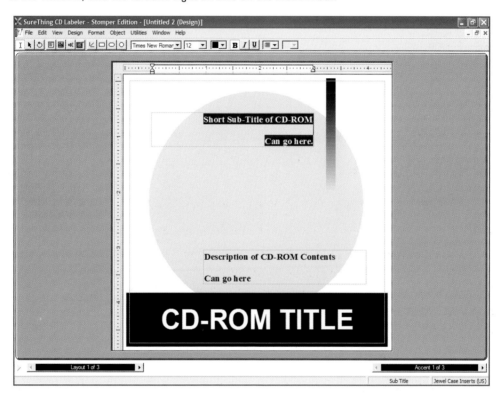

5. When you decide on a design, click any of the text boxes on-screen to enter the information you want to appear on the front of the insert.
6. To change the formatting for any text box, select the text, click the Format menu, and then select the formatting you want.
7. To add a picture or graphic image to the insert, click the Picture Tool button (or click the Object menu, choose Tools, and choose Picture Tool).
8. Draw a box where you want the image to appear using the program's drawing tools.
9. The New Picture dialog box opens. Select the image file you want to add to the label, and click OK.

7

10. To display the back of the insert, click the **View** menu and choose **Full Page**. This view displays your insert's front and back.
11. Click the **View** menu and choose **Actual Size** to better view the label.
12. Add and format the text in each text box, and add image files if desired.

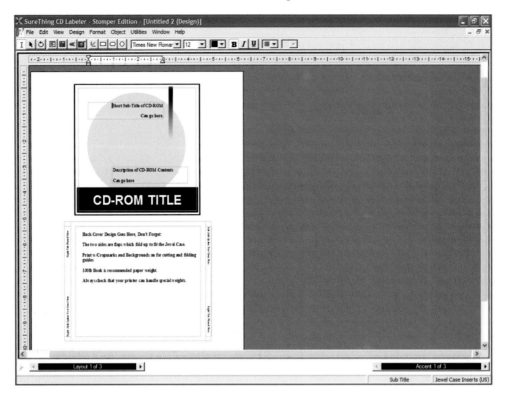

13. When you finish designing the insert, click the **File** menu and choose **Save As** to save your work to your desired location.
14. To print the insert, click the **File** menu and choose **Print**.

To Keep on Learning . . .

 Go to the CD-ROM and select the segment:
- *CD Burning Software* to learn about the features of popular CD burning software.

 Go online to **www.LearnwithGateway.com** and log on to select:
- *Roxio Easy CD Creator*
- *MusicMatch Jukebox*
- *Nero Burning ROM*
- *Internet Links and Resources*
  - *Analog to Digital Converting Software*
  - *CD-Recording Programs*
  - *CD-Labeling Programs*
  - *Home Audio Recording*
- *FAQs*

 Gateway offers a hands-on training course that covers many of the topics in this chapter. Additional fees may apply. Call **888-852-4821** for enrollment information. If applicable, please have your customer ID and order number ready when you call.

7

CHAPTER 8

Troubleshooting Scenarios

176   Resolving Internet-Connection Problems
> Put an end to connectivity troubles

178   Troubleshooting CD-Recording Problems
> Deal with burners that don't burn

186   Rectifying Music-Playback Problems
> Fix poor-quality sound and other playback predicaments

When you slip an audio CD into your CD player at home or in your car, you expect it to play high-quality sound with no skips, pops, or other defects. After all, the near-perfect quality of the audio CD format is one of the primary reasons CDs replaced albums and cassettes!

Unfortunately, however, you may occasionally encounter problems in the discs you record, such as poor sound quality. Even worse, there may be times when you have trouble playing the CDs you record at all. Alternatively, you may experience difficulties in the recording process that prevent you from burning your own CDs in the first place. In this chapter, you'll learn about some of the common problems people experience when burning their own CDs, and the simple things you can do to resolve them. First, however, you'll find out how to resolve some Internet-connection problems you may experience that prevent you from downloading music files from the Internet.

Resolving Internet-Connection Problems

If you can't download music files from the Internet, this could hinder your ability to expand your music collection. As a worst-case scenario, if your computer's Internet connection is completely broken—that is, you can't connect at all—take these simple steps to try to get your connection working:

1. Disconnect and re-connect your Internet link.
2. Double-check the dial-up phone number used by your Internet connection, and then try connecting again.
3. Double-check your logon user name and password, and then try connecting again.
4. Reboot your computer. Try connecting again.
5. Change the phone cord connecting your modem to the telephone jack on the wall. Try connecting again.

If these actions fail to establish a working connection, contact your ISP or online service provider to inquire about problems preventing you from obtaining normal Internet access. You may discover that some sort of outage is to blame. In that case, your best bet is to wait things out and try to establish your connection later.

Alternatively, you may find that you can connect to the Internet, but have difficulty actually downloading digital audio files. For example, you may be able to transfer the files to your hard drive, but they're damaged or corrupted. If so, it could be a problem with the digital files themselves. Try downloading another version of the same file and see if that works. Alternatively, it could be the result of a glitch with your Internet connection. In that case, try disconnecting and then reconnecting to your Internet service provider or online service provider. Alternatively, try to attempt your download during a less-busy time of day.

If the process of downloading digital music files works, but seems to take hours to complete, your Internet connection is simply too slow. (A slow connection will also cause poor-quality streaming audio playback.) There are a few ways to fix this problem, but the most effective way is to upgrade your dial-up connection to a high-speed alternative such as cable or DSL (Digital Subscriber Line). If upgrading your connection speed is not an option, there are still a few actions you can take, but improvements gained by these actions are usually minimal:

✦ Disconnect and reconnect until you get a higher connection speed (i.e., close to or over 28.8 Kbps).

✦ Wait until non-peak hours to dial-in. Peak hours are typically 3–8 P.M. weekdays.

✦ Reboot your computer and re-connect.

Another reason you may have difficulties downloading files from the Internet is that a firewall or proxy governs your Internet connection. Firewalls and proxies provide security to systems connected to the Internet. In most cases, when you're downloading files directly from a Web page, a firewall or proxy will not hamper the download. However, if you're using a specialized peer-sharing tool, a firewall or proxy could very well be preventing its use. If you suspect that the firewall or proxy is preventing you from downloading files, contact the vendor of that product for help. If however, you're encountering problems while on a work computer, contact the system administrator in charge of maintaining the firewall or proxy system.

8

Troubleshooting CD-Recording Problems

When it comes to recording your own CDs, you may discover that it's not always as seamless a process as you'd like. In fact, almost everyone who's enjoyed burning their own CDs has ruined their fair share of discs (fortunately, they make lovely coasters and mobiles). To avoid common CD-recording pitfalls, keep the following points in mind:

✦ Make sure the speed range for the recordable discs you purchase matches or exceeds the speed range for your recordable drive.

 When selecting discs, read the package to determine the speed rating for the discs. To determine the speed of your drive, check your computer or CD drive manual.

✦ If you have trouble burning files onto 80-minute discs, use 74-minute discs instead.

✦ Once you start a copy or burn operation, leave your computer alone. Don't run any programs, and avoid moving near your computer. Motion can cause slight vibrations in the recorder that might negatively affect the copying operation.

✦ For optimal results, your CD recorder should be the *only* program running on your computer. Other programs can interfere with transferring the digital data you're trying to record. Close any programs running on your machine (except, of course, the CD-recording software), including those programs running in the background. Exiting programs frees up more memory for recording CDs and prevents background programs from interfering with the copy operation. Exiting background programs can get tricky, so you might want to get some help from an expert.

 If the recording process stops and starts intermittently, you probably have other programs running on your computer.

To ensure that your CD burner has enough room on the hard drive to temporarily store files while writing to the recordable disc, use Windows XP's Disk Cleanup feature to delete any files that are no longer needed on your system. For help using Disk Cleanup, refer to Windows XP's Help system. In addition, to speed up your hard drive, you can *defragment* it using Windows XP's Disk Defragmenter utility. Again, refer to Windows XP's Help system for instructions.

When you defragment your hard drive, the files are made contiguous instead of being fragmented. A fragmented drive can degrade performance.

If you've adhered to these guidelines and your CD burner still doesn't record as expected, try the following:

1 Make sure you have a blank CD-R disc in your recordable CD drive. You can't record over a CD-R disc you previously recorded.

2 To determine whether the problem is with your burner or the files you're trying to record, try previewing the files before you record them. Most CD-recording programs offer a preview button, which you can click to play a song to make sure it's not corrupt before you try to record it. Easy CD Creator from Roxio has this feature. If you can't preview the song, try recording some different files. If these files copy correctly, the problem stems from the original files, which are likely damaged or corrupted in some way. To resolve the problem, try to obtain new copies of the original files by downloading them from another source or re-copying them to your hard drive from CD.

Preview button

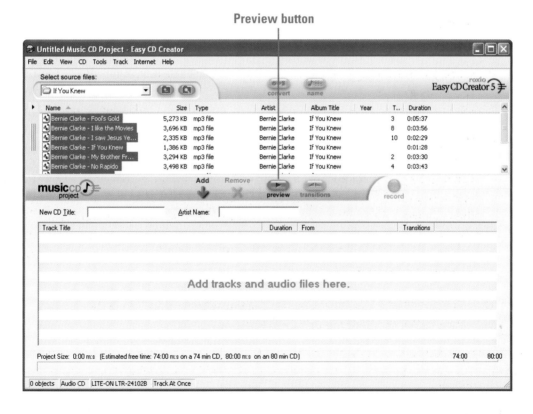

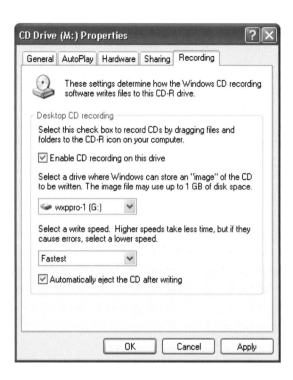

❸ If the problem lies with your CD burner, it may be because the CD drive is trying to burn the new CD at too high a speed. Try selecting a slower write speed. In Windows XP My Computer, right-click the icon for your recordable disc drive and choose **Properties**. Click the **Recording** tab, display the Write speed drop-down list, choose the next slower speed, and click **OK**.

 Lowering the speed means it will take your drive longer to create the new CD, but the risk for errors is minimized.

More About . . . Roxio and Write Speed

If you have Roxio Easy CD Creator installed, the tab will be named DirectCD 5.0 Options and this option is not available on this tab. You need to open Easy CD Creator and choose **Tools**, **CD Drive Properties** and change the Write speed there.

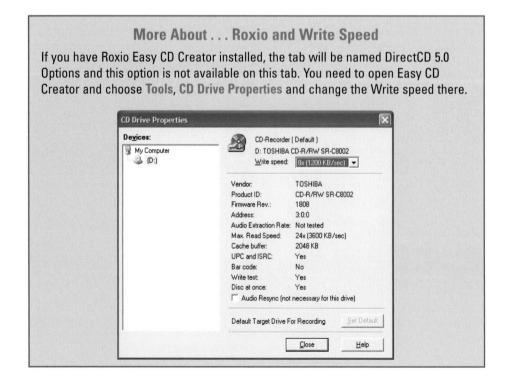

If you have added a CD-RW to an older system, make sure the processor and RAM exceed the minimum requirements. Otherwise, the burner may not work correctly. For example, if you install a 24x CD-RW drive on a 200 MHz machine, it most likely will not record smoothly at that speed.

Still having problems? It could be because your computer doesn't recognize your CD drive or CD-recording software. The next two sections help you resolve those frustrating problems.

Ensuring Your Computer Recognizes Your CD Drive

If you've completed the steps outlined in the preceding section and your CD drive still won't record, you'll want to determine whether your system actually recognizes your recordable CD-ROM drive. To do so in Windows XP, follow these steps:

1. Click the **start** button and click **Control Panel**.
2. Control Panel opens. Click **Performance and Maintenance**.
3. In the Performance and Maintenance window, click the **System** icon. The System Properties dialog box opens.

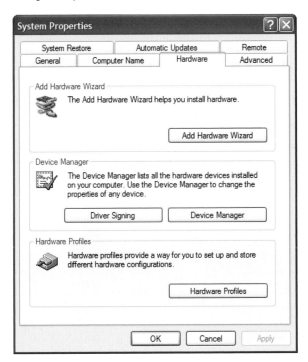

4. Click the **Hardware** tab to select it.
5. Click the **Device Manager** button.

8

6 The Device Manager window opens. Expand the DVD/CD-ROM drive section to view the list of known CD/DVD drives (this will include both recordable and non-recordable drives). If no CD/DVD drive entry exists, stop here and proceed to the paragraphs following this exercise for more information.

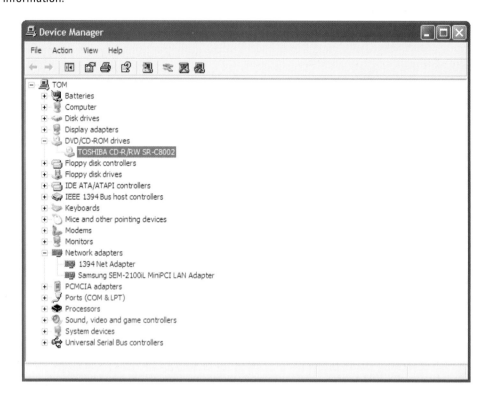

 If multiple CD/DVD drives are installed on your computer, multiple items will appear within the DVD/CD-ROM drive section. Your CD burner drive should be listed with a CD-R or CD-RW in its name. If not, you'll need to know the exact model number (see your packing slip or purchase invoice).

7 Once you locate the drive, double-click on it. The drive's Properties dialog box opens.

8 From the General tab of the drive's Properties dialog box, click the **Troubleshoot** button to launch the Troubleshooting Wizard. This wizard walks you through a problem resolution process step-by-step. Just follow the directions and answer the questions on each page of the wizard.

If your computer doesn't recognize its recordable CD drive in step 6, it could simply be because something isn't connected properly. This is especially likely if you've just installed the drive. Before you do anything else, check all the cables and connections to make sure everything is firmly connected to the right connectors.

After you verify that everything is connected properly and your recordable CD drive is still not working, the likely culprit is a missing or damaged driver. A *driver* is a piece of software that Windows uses to access a specific piece of hardware (in this case, a recordable CD drive). Most drivers are included on the hardware's installation CD, and are installed automatically when the hardware is installed and configured.

8

If there's any sort of problem with your CD drive or driver, an exclamation-point icon will appear next to the drive's entry in Device Manager. To try to resolve this problem, double-click on the device's icon in the Device Manager to open its Properties dialog box, and then click the **Driver** tab. From this tab, you can perform three actions: Update Driver, Roll Back Driver, and Uninstall. First and foremost, you should try to Uninstall the driver and reboot. Windows XP will automatically detect and re-install the CD/DVD device; however, you may be prompted for device drivers.

 You can also right-click the device and choose **Uninstall**.

The other options available on the Driver tab are as follows:

✦ **Update Driver.** Use this to install a new driver for the device. This command can search for a new driver on local floppies, CDs, folders on your hard drive, or from the Microsoft Windows Update Web site. If there's a new driver provided by the manufacturer on their Web site, it should be downloaded to your computer before using this command.

✦ **Roll Back Driver.** Use this to remove the current driver and return to the previous driver. This command is only useful if you've updated to a new driver and the new driver doesn't work.

You should reboot your system after performing any of these options. If these processes fail to remove the exclamation point icon from the CD/DVD device, there's usually something more wrong with the system than just a missing device driver. You may need to get professional help to resolve the problem. Consult the user manual for the CD/DVD drive and contact a professional repair technician for aid.

Ensuring Your Computer Recognizes Your CD-Recording Software

Suppose you're having trouble with the recording software installed on your machine. Specifically, you can't get it to run. If so, there are a few possible culprits.

One possibility is that you may be trying to use an older program with a newer computer or operating system. For example, if you had an older version of Roxio's Easy CD Creator installed on your computer, and then upgraded your computer to Windows XP, you probably found that Easy CD Creator didn't work anymore. To solve this problem, you'd need to upgrade to a newer version of the software—specifically, one that's compatible with your version of Windows.

If you've upgraded your software, and it still doesn't work, try uninstalling it and then reinstalling it. On rare occasions, new software installations don't "take," and must be repeated to work properly.

Still at a loss? In that case, check with the software manufacturer's Web site to see if what you're experiencing is a known problem that affects your particular installation. Some programs have bugs that cause them not to work properly in certain circumstances. In most cases, when a software manufacturer is alerted of a bug, it develops and distributes a fix for it. (A *fix*, sometimes called a *patch*, is a program designed to resolve a known software problem.) You can then download the fix and install it on your computer to fix the bug and get the software up and running.

8

Rectifying Music-Playback Problems

You may occasionally encounter problems in the discs you record, such as poor sound quality. (Likewise, poor sound quality may sometimes be an issue when you listen to streaming audio.) Even worse, there may be times when you have trouble playing the CDs you record at all. In this section, you learn some simple steps you can take to resolve these issues.

Fixing Poor Sound Quality

As you listen to your digital recordings, you may encounter stutters or gurgles in the sound. If it's a gurgle you hear, there's a good chance the file itself is damaged or corrupted. Try downloading the file again; if that doesn't resolve the problem, find another source for the file. The same advice holds true if you get an MP3 or WMA file with lots of beeps, crackles, and erratic volume.

 If you have a poor-sounding MP3 or WMA file, it could be because of the bit rate you chose for the recording. Low bit-rate recordings can sound very compressed, kind of like a song played over AM radio. Unfortunately, you cannot fix this problem within the copy of the song you already have. You must re-record the song at (or download a version of the song with) a higher bit rate for better sound quality.

If you hear a stutter, the likely cause is that your system is overloaded. This will affect playback. This typically happens when you're using your computer to do several things at once—download a big file from the Internet, perform a complex spreadsheet calculation, send and receive e-mail, and listen to digital music. To solve this problem, simply close one or more competing programs. Alternatively, as a long-term solution, consider increasing your computer's memory.

You may also experience sound-quality problems when listening to streaming audio, especially if you use dial-up to connect to the Internet. These problems are typically because of the speed (or lack thereof) of your Internet connection. To ensure the highest-quality uninterrupted streaming-media performance, you really need a broadband DSL or cable modem connection.

A typical streaming-audio sound problem is unwanted pauses and stuttering in the program's playback. This happens when the player plays the data in the buffer before it can download enough of the rest of the file to keep playing. If your player consistently empties its buffer, which can happen a lot with a slower dial-up Internet connection, you should increase the buffer's size (usually measured in seconds of playback); therefore, allowing the player to download more of the audio data before it begins playback. (Alternatively, upgrade to a faster Internet connection.)

> ### More About . . . Buffers
>
> As you learned in Chapter 6, streaming audio players work by playing the first part of the recording before they finish downloading the rest of the audio file. This process gathers the first part of the audio stream in a *buffer*, or storage area on your hard disk. When the buffer is full, the audio starts playing as the player continues to download the rest of the audio file.

To increase the buffer size in Windows Media Player, do the following:

 If you use a different streaming-audio player, consult its help documentation for information about increasing buffer size.

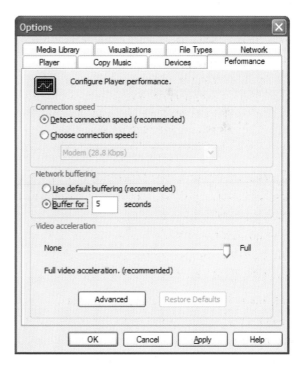

❶ In the Windows Media Player program window, click the **Tools** menu and choose **Options**.

❷ The Options dialog box opens. Click the **Performance** tab.

❸ Select the **Buffer for *XX* seconds** radio button in the Network buffering section.

❹ Define a buffer size in seconds of playback time.

❺ Click **OK**.

 If you find that streaming files are simply taking too long to start playing back, it's likely because your computer's buffer is too large. To rectify this in Windows Media Player, perform the proceeding steps but set the buffer size to a smaller number. This tells the player to download fewer seconds of the media file before it begins playback.

8

Enabling Playback

Even worse than a CD with poor-quality sound is a CD with no sound at all. If your attempts to play your CD are in vain, consider the following:

✦ Make sure the disc you want to play and the drive in which you want to play it are compatible. You can't play CD-RW discs in most regular CD or DVD players or in most CD-R drives. In addition, some older CD players and DVD drives can't handle certain CD-R discs.

✦ Make sure the CD is in good shape. If the bottom of the CD is scratched, or has liquid spilled on it, the disc may be so damaged you can't play it. (Water's okay, as long as you wipe it off; other liquids can leave a residue.) Also make sure that if there's a label on the CD, it's firmly attached. Loose labels can gum up the disc's rotation. If the disc itself is warped, you may not be able to play it.

 CD-R and CD-RW discs, while very durable, aren't *quite* as durable as commercial audio CDs. Extreme heat, direct sunlight, spilled liquids, and the like can more easily damage recordable discs than manufactured ones.

If neither of these solutions works, there's a strong chance you can't play the CD because it encountered a problem during recording, or because the files it contains are damaged or corrupted. Re-read the section "Troubleshooting CD-Recording Problems" earlier in this chapter for advice on resolving these issues.

To Keep on Learning . . .

Go online to **www.LearnwithGateway.com** and log on to select:
- *Internet Links and Resources*
- *FAQs*

With the *Survive & Thrive* series, refer to *Communicate and Connect to the Internet* for more information on:
- *Average speed of the different types of Internet connections*

Gateway offers a hands-on training course that covers many of the topics in this chapter. Additional fees may apply. Call **888-852-4821** for enrollment information. If applicable, please have your customer ID and order number ready when you call.

8

Glossary

adware   Programs that can be used for free but that occasionally display advertisements or collect information about your surfing habits.

analog   Sounds created continuously, without any breaks used to carry information (such as by modems over telephone lines) or produce audio (such as with some speakers).

anti-virus   A program that continually scans your system for any sign of virus infection. These types of programs can also scan each file you download to make sure it's not infected.

blank   A new CD-R or an erased CD-RW that is ready to be written to.

broadband   A type of network connection that can support a wide range of transmission frequencies. In other words, a connection medium that can support multiple simultaneous connections. For example, cable modems and DSL are broadband technologies used to gain Internet access.

buffer   A designated area of memory that playback and recording devices use to pre-load material in order to maintain a consistent stream of data to the player or recorder.

CD-R   A write-once form of CD media. If you have a CD-R (compact disc-recordable) drive, you can write data to CD-R media, but you can only write to CD-R media once. Once a CD-R media is burned, it can be read in any type of CD or DVD drive. Audio CDs created from CD-Rs can usually be played in your home or car CD player. Also called recordable CDs.

CD-ROM   A CD or a CD-ROM media is a read-only CD (hence the name ROM, or read only memory). This means you can only read data from the CD; you cannot write data to the CD. Any type of CD or DVD drive can read CD-ROM media.

CD-RW   A write-many-times form of CD media. If you have a CD-RW (compact disc-rewritable) drive, you can write data to CD-R or CD-RW media. You can still only write once to a CD-R media, but you can write, erase, and write data onto CD-RW media again and again. Once a CD-RW media is burned, it can be read in any type of CD drive. Often, audio CDs created from CD-RWs can be played in your home or car CD player. Also called rewriteable CDs.

client   The system that requests a resource, such as a file or a streaming multimedia presentation, from a server.

commercial   When referring to software, this is a type of program that must be purchased before it can be used.

compressed   The state of an audio file that has been reduced in size, commonly without noticeable loss in sound quality.

compression   The act of reducing an audio file in size, commonly without noticeable loss in sound quality.

copyright   A set of laws designed to make sure that the person who creates something (a piece of art, a computer program, a Web site, a movie, or a piece of music) is protected from other people claiming it as their own.

CPU   The main processor chip on a computer's motherboard—not the whole system unit (a common, but mistaken, use of the term).

data compression   A way to make a file smaller, while still retaining much of the original quality. Data compression is used to conserve storage space or improve transmission time.

defragment   The process of making the files on your computer contiguous rather than fragmented. A fragmented drive can degrade performance.

digital bits   An electronic equivalent of a 1 or a 0 that represents small bursts of information. A stream of digital bits can be used to represent an audio signal or computer communications over a wire.

DVD   A DVD (digital versatile disc) media is a read-only DVD. You can play a movie DVD in your home theatre DVD player or in the DVD drive on your computer. A DVD media can be played in any type of DVD drive.

DVD-R   A write-once form of DVD media. A DVD-R (digital versatile disc-recordable) media is a DVD media that can be written to once. A DVD-R or DVD-RAM drive is required to write to DVD-R media. Once a DVD-R is burned, it can be read in any type of DVD drive.

DVD-RAM   A write-many-times form of DVD media. You can write, erase, and write data again to a DVD-RAM media with a DVD-RAM drive. Once a DVD-RAM is burned, it can be read in any type of DVD drive.

dynamic range   The difference between the loudest and softest sounds produced by an audio device.

file format   The method used to store data in a file. Different types of programs use different file formats. For example, audio programs use audio file formats, and word processors use document file formats.

find   The process of searching for something either locally or over the Internet, such as people, songs, or programs.

freeware   Programs designated by their authors to be used freely by anyone without charge.

Internet radio   Live audio broadcasts that can be listened to using a streaming audio player. Also called *Webcasting*.

line in port   The jack on a sound card that accepts incoming signals from an external audio source, such as a radio, external CD player, or even another computer.

microphone in port   The jack on a sound card that accepts a microphone.

oscilloscope   A tool used to measure waves, such as sound wave and electronic waves.

PDA (personal digital assistant)   A portable computer designed to act as an organizer, note taker, communication device, and so forth. PDAs are fast, functional, and include various user-friendly applications to help you organize business and personal activities.

peer   A computer system that has the same functionality and access as yours.

P2P (peer-to-peer) file-sharing   A means by which users can swap files with other people on the Internet. All of the computers participating in P2P file sharing are *peers* to each other and neither functions as a dedicated server, as with a traditional Web site. You can pull files from other people's computers and they can pull files from your computer.

quantization   The size of each digital sample in a recording, measured in bits.

RAM   Temporarily stores data, software, and the operating system while a computer is operating; everything in RAM is temporary.

recordable   *See CD-R.*

rewritable   *See CD-RW.*

ripping   The process of creating a digital audio file on your computer's hard drive from a song on a music CD.

sampling   The process of converting analog sound to digital bits.

sampling rate   The number of samples are taken per second from an audio source.

shareware   Programs designated by their authors to be freely used only for a designated evaluation period, after which they require a fee and registration before legal, continued use is granted.

signal-to-noise ratio   The ratio of the actual sound you hear compared to the high background noise.

spyware   Programs that hide in the background while you're connected for file-swapping and collect information about your surfing habits.

streaming audio   A delivery means by which a multimedia presentation can be played while it continues to download.

streaming audio player   Multimedia software that can be installed onto your computer. This is a type of computer program that enables you to listen to a sound file even before it's finished downloading to your machine or, in the case of Internet radio, to listen to a continuous sound file.

subscription music services   Internet sites that enable users to download multimedia files for a fee.

universal access   The capability to access something anywhere, any time, with little or no change in quality or service.

visualizations   Cool-looking graphics that may move in time to the music and appear on most media players.

Index

3D Audio, 43
3D audio support (surround sound), 43, 45, 46

A

AAC file format, 64, 66, 70
adware, 125, 127
AMG (All Music Guide), 107, 109
amplifiers. *See* home stereos
analog
    basic description of, 3–5
    copying, from CDs, 157–158
    recording, with a microphone, 167–168
anti-virus software, 126. *See also* viruses
AOL Time Warner, 102
archives. *See* audio archives
Audigy, 45
audio archives, 98–100
Audio Home Recording Act, 32, 33
Audiogalaxy, 123

B

background noise, 5, 8, 16
BearShare, 124
Berne Convention, 28–29, 33
Bertelsmann, 102
bit rates, 186
BMG Entertainment, 102
boom boxes, 20
broadband connections, 10, 104, 105, 115, 177
browser(s)
    downloading files with, 105–106
    file sharing and, 123
    Internet Explorer, 105–106, 117
Internet radio and, 113–114, 117
    plug-ins, 114
buffers, 186–187
Burner Plus, 146–147
burning CDs, 48–52, 132, 141–158, 165–166. *See also* recording
    with digital music players, 137–138, 141–145
    duplicating entire CDs, 155–157
    copying LPs and cassettes to CDs, 157–158
    mechanical processes involved with, 132–133
    use of the term, 48

C

cable access, to the Internet, 10, 105, 115
cables. *See* connectors
car, digital audio players for, 22, 57
cassette tapes, 16, 17, 21, 32, 157–165
CD Copier, 155–157
CD Stomper, 168–172
CD Writing Wizard, 155
CDA file format, 64, 66, 141, 143
CDDB, 107, 108, 109, 113
CD-ROM, 48, 51, 70, 79, 133, 136, 139, 152. *See also* CDs (compact discs)
CD-ROM drive, 48, 51, 113, 181–182
CD-R, 48, 50–51, 133–134
CD-R drives
    described, 48–50
    duplicating entire CDs with, 155–157
recording audio CDs with, 141–152
    recording MP3 CDs with, 152–155
    speed of, 51–52
    troubleshooting, 178–184, 188.
    See also CD-RW drives; CDs (compact discs)
CD-RW, 49–51
CD-RW drives, 49–51, 135–136, 188. *See also* CD-R drives; CDs (compact discs)
CDs (compact discs)
    CDA file format and, 64, 66, 141, 143
    condition of, 188
    copying LPs and cassettes to, 157–158
    copying music from, to your hard drive, 78–80
    copying music between, 152
    duplicating entire, 155–157
    jewel cases for, 136, 168, 171–172
    labels for, 168–170, 188
    mass-producing, 52
    media, 6, 9, 48, 50–51, 133–135
    MP3, 141, 152–155
    multi-session, 140
    problems with, troubleshooting, 178–179
    speed ratings for, 178, 180
    storage space on, 9–10
    taking care of, 136
    See also burning CDs; CD-R drives; CD-RW drives
cell phones, 57
Click 'N Burn Pro, 138

client software programs, 124
Collectorz.com, 113
compression, 10, 63, 65, 96–97, 152
computer(s)
    baseline electronic noise created by, 44
    connecting home stereos to, 45, 53–54, 157–158
    laptop, 49
    loading music into portable music players from, 55
    recognition of CD drives by, 181–184
    recognition of recording software by, 185
    rebooting, 176, 177, 184
    system requirements, 41
    system unit case, 42
connectors
    basic description of, 44
    connection-type mismatches and, 53–54
    gold-plated, 54
    troubleshooting, 183
    See also ports
consumer rights, 32–33
copy protection, 66
copyright, 24, 27–36
    corporations and, 29, 31–32
copyright holders rights, 28–33
copyright law, 24, 27–36, 119–120
Copyright Office Web site, 34–35
CPUs (central processing units), 41
Creative Labs, 43, 45

D

data compression, 10, 63, 65, 96–97, 152
databases, 107–109
dB SN Ratio (decibel signal to noise ratio), 44, 47
decompression, of files, 86–87.
    See also data compression

deframentation, 178–179
Device Manager, 181–184
dial-up connections, 10, 176, 177, 186
dielectric layer, 135
digital audio archives. *See* audio archives
Digital Millennium Copyright Act (DMCA), 29
digital music players
    all-in-one, 69, 75
    burning CDs with, 137–138, 141–145
    choosing, 67–77
    downloading, 76–77
    icons for, 77
    installing, 76–77
    playing music with, 77–83, 87–88
    playlists, 19, 68, 69, 83, 87–88, 112–113, 141, 146
    portable, 21–22, 45, 54–57
    registering, 77
    searching online databases with, 107
    shuffle feature, 88
    skins for, 68, 89–90
    visualizations generated by, 71, 72, 73, 74
    See also MusicMatch Jukebox, Media Player (Windows)
Digital Subscriber Line (DSL), 10, 104, 105, 115, 177
Digital Video Recorders, 23
DirectAudio, 43
directories. *See* folders
DirectX architecture, 43
Disk Cleanup, 178
DJ mixers, 76
docking modules, 57
Dolby Digital sound, 45, 46
downloading
    digital music players, 76–77
    skins, 89
    software fixes/patches, 185
    See also downloading music

downloading music, 19, 23–24, 68
    from audio archives, 98–100
    basic description of, 105–106
    file sharing and, 120–121
    security issues related to, 125–126
    from subscription music services, 101–105
    speed of, 10, 105
    troubleshooting, 176–177
drivers, 183–184
DSL (Digital Subscriber Line), 10, 104, 105, 115, 177
DVD, 49–51, 136, 138
DVD (digital versatile disc) drives
    selecting, 48–50
    speed of, 51–52
    troubleshooting, 182–184, 188
    types of, 49–51

E

Easy CD Creator (Roxio), 141, 148–153, 155–158
    basic description of, 138
    CD Copier, 155–157
    creating labels with, 168
    preview feature, 179
    recording WAV files with, 161–166
    troubleshooting, 185
    write speed and, 180
EAX file format, 43
Echo Web site, 118
Edison, Thomas, 2, 4
EMI Group, 102, 104
EMusic service, 101–102
encoding, 10, 69–70, 72, 78–79
exclamation-point icon, 184
executable programs, 126
expansion cards, 42, 43–44
external cards, 45, 53
Extigy, 45
Extraction Wizard, 97

F

FastTrack technology, 124
file(s)
  copy-protected, 66
  compression, 10, 63, 65,
    96–97, 152
  -name extensions, 64–65, 126
  organizing, 110–113
  storing, 110–111, 119–124,
    127, 125
  See also file formats
file formats
  described, 62–67, 96–97
  digital music players and, 54,
    70
  streaming audio and,
    115–116
  See also AAC, CDA, EAX,
    LQT, MIDI, MPC,
    MP3, RA, RM, VQF,
    WAV, and WMA
firewalls, 118, 177
FireWire ports, 45, 55
fixes, 185
FM synthesis, 43
folders
  copying files from, 153–154
  My Documents folder, 107
  My Music folder, 64, 81, 107,
    110–111
  saving files in, 107
  storing files in, 110–111
freeware, 69–70
frequency response, 47
full duplex sound, 44

G

games, 44, 109
Gnutella, 123–124
Gracenote, 108
gradations, 3

H

hard drive(s)
  copying music from CDs to,
    78–80

defragmenting, 178–179
  for portable music players, 56,
    57
  requirements, for optimal
    performance, 41
  searching, for audio files,
    83–84
  viruses and, 125, 126
hardware
  basic description of, 40–58
  drivers, 183–184
  requirements, 41
  troubleshooting, 178–181,
    184
  See also specific devices
headphones, 44
help, 178
home stereo(s)
  connecting your computer to,
    45, 53–54, 157–158
  copying analog media from,
    to CDs, 157–158
  jacks, 44, 53–55
  turntables, 4, 157–158
  See also cassette tapes; vinyl
    records

I

IEEE (Institute of Electronics
    and Electrical Engineers)
    1394 ports, 45, 55
integrated sound card, 42
Internet
  cable access to, 10, 105, 115
  connection problems,
    troubleshooting,
    176–177
  dial-up access to, 10, 176,
    177, 186
  DSL access to, 10, 104, 105,
    115, 177
  radio, 104, 113–119
Internet Explorer browser,
    105–106, 117. *See also*
    browsers

ISA (Industry Standard
    Architecture) slots, 52
ISP (Internet Service Provider),
    107

J

jewel cases, 136, 168, 171–172
  inserts for, 137, 168, 171

K

KaZaA network, 124

L

labels, for CDs, 168–170, 188
lands, defined, 132
laptop computers, 49. *See also*
    computers
LearnwithGateway.com, 12
Library of Congress, 33–35
licensing, 66, 101
LimeWire, 124
line in connection, 44
line out connection, 44
Liquid Player, 70, 75
LPs. *See* vinyl records
LQT file format, 64, 66, 70

M

"May Not Fit" message,
    144–145
McAfee VirusScan, 126
media
  -duplication companies, 52
  use of the term, 51
Media Player (Windows),
    19–20, 66
  buffer size settings, 187
  burning audio CDs with,
    141–145
  changing views in, 88–89
  copying music from CDs to
    your hard drive with,
    78–80
  described, 70–72, 78
  downloading files with, 107
  Internet radio and, 118

learning more about, 85
Media Guide, 107
Media Library, 80, 83–86
playing music with, 80–81,
    87–88
playlist, 19, 87–88, 83,
    87–88, 110, 112–113,
    141–144, 146–147
Radio Tuner, 22, 118
skins, 89–90
sorting music files with, 86
volume adjustments, 82
memory
cards, 54, 55–56, 57
for portable digital music
    players, 21
requirements, 41
microphones, 41, 44, 167
Microsoft Network (MSN), 103
Microsoft Sound Recorder, 158,
    159–162, 167–168
Microsoft Windows XP. *See*
    Windows XP
    (Microsoft)
MIDI file format, 44, 64,
    66–67, 70
mid-range woofers, 47, 48
modems, 115, 176
motherboard, 42
movies. *See* DVDs (digital
    versatile disc) drives;
    videos
MP3 files, 22, 63–67, 70
audio archives and, 98
converting WAV files to, 158
data compression and, 10
downloading, 105–106
file extensions and, 126
file sharing and, 121–122
recording, 78–79, 141,
    152–155
sound-quality problems
    related to, 186–187
streaming, 115, 116
subscription sites and,
    101–103

MP3 CD Maker, 138
MP3 Creation Pack, 78
MP3.com, 99, 103
MPC file format, 64
MPEGplus, 65
MSN (Microsoft Network), 103
music
libraries, 112–113
-management software, 113
services, subscription, 23, 98,
    101–105
Music Collector, 113
music players. *See* digital music
    players; playing music
music search site, 23, 100
MusicCity Morpheus, 124
MusicMatch Jukebox, 70, 85
basic description of, 72–73,
    88–89
burning audio CDs with,
    146–148
creating MP3 CDs with, 153
downloading/installing,
    76–77
playlists, 87
MusicNet, 101, 102, 103, 104
My Computer, 153, 154, 180
My Documents folder, 107
My Music folder, 64, 81, 107,
    110–111

N

Napster, 28, 102, 121–122
Nero Burning ROM, 138–139,
    141, 168
normalizing, 166
Norton AntiVirus, 126
Notepad (Microsoft), 62

O

omni-directional sound, 46
online databases, 107–109
Open dialog box, 81, 85
oscilloscope, 3

P

P2P (peer-to-peer) file sharing,
    119–125, 127
pagers, 57
passwords, 176
patches, 185
PCI (Peripheral Component
    Interconnect) slots, 42,
    43
PCM format, 160
PDAs (personal digital
    assistants), 23, 57
peer-to-peer file sharing. *See* P2P
    (peer-to-peer) file
    sharing
Pfleumer, Fritz, 4
Philips Company, 5
phonograph, 2, 4
pits, 132, 133
playing music, 77–83, 87–88
from audio CDs, 19–20
controls for, 71, 78, 81–82
from selected folders, 111
sound-quality problems
    related to, 186–187
troubleshooting, 186–188
See also digital music players;
    playlists
playlists, 19, 68, 69, 83
creating, 87–88
described, 112–113
generating, when recording
    audio CDs, 141, 146
shuffle feature, 88
See also playing music
plug-ins, 114
portable digital music players,
    21–22, 45
described, 54–57
loading music into, 55
two types of, 55–56
See also digital music players
ports.
FireWire, 45, 55
USB (Universal Serial Bus),
    45, 55

See also connectors

press*play,* 101, 103, 104

printing

jewel case inserts, 172

labels, 170

processors, 41

Q

quantization, 6, 7, 8

QuickTime, 115

QuickTime player, 115

R

RA (RealAudio) format, 64, 67, 70

radio, Internet, 104, 113–119

RAM (Random Access Memory). *See* memory

RCA jacks, 54

Real Networks, 74, 102, 104, 115–117

RealAudio, 115–117. *See also* RA (RealAudio) format

RealJukebox, 74

RealOne, 101, 102, 104

RealOne Player, 70, 74, 104, 116, 117

RealPlayer, 74

rebooting, 176, 177, 184

receivers. *See* home stereos

recording

analog, 2–5

analog sounds, 167–168

audio CDs, 140–152

basic description of, 6, 16–18, 131–173

CD formats for, 132–135

copyright law and, 27–36

errors, 179, 180

finalize, 151

history of, 2–5, 16

with Media Player, 78–80

methods, configuring, 140

with microphones, 167–168

MP3 files, 78–79, 141, 152–155

preparing your system for, 139

quality, 160, 162–165

software, 137–139

sound cleaning features and, 162–165

speed ratings for, 160, 178, 180

test, 140

track-by-track, 140

troubleshooting, 144–145, 178–185

WAV files, 159–164

See also burning CDs

records (LPs). *See* vinyl records

resolution, of sound samples, 160

RIAA (Recording Industry Association of America), 28

ripping, 17, 69, 70. *See also* recording

RM (RealMedia) file format, 64, 70

Roxio Web site, 103. *See also* Easy CD Creator (Roxio)

royalty, 31

S

sampling, 6–8, 10, 11, 17

sampling rates, 6–7, 8, 17, 64–66, 79, 160

security

file sharing and, 122, 125

firewalls and, 118, 177

passwords, 176

servers, 120–121, 123

shareware, 69–70, 137

sharing files, 119–125, 127

SHOUTcast technology, 116

shuffle feature, 88

signal-to-noise ratio, 8, 44, 47

skins, 68, 89–90

Sony, 21, 103

sorting files, 86–87

sound

cards, 40–45, 46, 47, 53–54

cleaning features, 162–165

immersion, 46

omni-directional, 46

sampling rates, 6–7, 8, 17, 65, 160

signal-to-noise ratio for, 8, 44, 47

surround, 43, 45, 46

Sound Recorder (Microsoft), 158, 159–162, 167–168

SoundBlaster sound cards, 43

SoundStream, 158, 161–166

speakers

power ratings for, 47

quality of, 40

selecting, 46–48

surround sound and, 43, 46

Spin Doctor, 158, 161–164

spyware, 125, 127

stereos. *See* home stereos

streaming audio, 11, 20, 67, 70, 103

file formats, 115–116

firewalls and, 118

Internet radio and, 113–119

sound-quality problems related to, 186–187

sub-woofers, 43, 46–47

subscription music services, 23, 98, 101–105

surround sound, 43, 45, 46

system requirements, 41

system tray, 82

T

taskbar, 82

THX specification, 45

TiVo, 23

training courses, 12

Troubleshooting Wizard, 183

turntables, 4, 157–158. *See also* home stereos

tweeters, 48

U

Universal Music, 103
upgrades, 185
URLs (Uniform Resource
        Locators), 85, 127
USB (Universal Serial Bus)
        ports, 45, 55

V

videos, 23, 104, 107. *See also*
        DVDs (digital versatile
        disc) drives
vinyl records, 4–5, 17, 157–162,
        165–166. *See also* home
        stereos
viruses, 125–126
visualizations, 71, 72, 73, 74
volume adjustments, 82
VQF file format, 64

W

Warner Music Group, 102, 104
WAV files, 63, 64, 67, 70
    conversion to, 141, 143, 158
    recording, 158–166
    sound cleaning features and,
        165–166
wave table synthesis, 43
Web browsers. *See* browsers

Web servers, 120–121, 123
Webcasting. *See* streaming audio
Winamp, 70, 73, 78, 116
Windows Media Player. *See*
        Media Player
        (Windows)
Windows XP (Microsoft)
    Control Panel, 82, 181
    creating MP3 CDs with,
        153–155
    Device Manager, 181–184
    Disk Cleanup, 178
    Disk Deframenter, 178–179
    downloading files with,
        105–106
    Extraction Wizard, 97
    folders, storing files in,
        110–111
    help system, 178
    inclusion of Windows Media
        Player with, 78
    Internet radio and, 116–117
    Troubleshooting Wizard, 183
    upgrades to, 185
    viewing file extensions with,
        64–65
WindowsMedia.com, 107, 118
WIPO (World Intellectual
        Property Organization),
        29

WMA files, 63–66, 70–71,
        78–79
    converting WAV files to, 158
    file extensions and, 126
    licensing features for, 66, 101
    MP3 CDs and, 152
    sound-quality problems
        related to, 186–187
    streaming audio and, 115,
        116
woofers, 47, 48
Word (Microsoft), 62–63
write speed, 178, 180

X

XM Radio, 23

Y

Yahoo!, 103
Yamaha, 51

Z

ZIP drives, 111
ZIP files, 96. *See also* data
        compression
Zomba, 102, 104

GATEWAY, INC. END-USER LICENSE AGREEMENT

IMPORTANT - READ CAREFULLY: This End-User License Agreement (EULA) is a legal agreement between you (either an individual or an entity), the End-User, and Gateway, Inc. ("Gateway") governing your use of any non-Microsoft software you acquired from Gateway collectively, the "SOFTWARE PRODUCT".

The SOFTWARE PRODUCT includes computer software, the associated media, any printed materials, and any "online" or electronic documentation. By turning on the system, opening the shrinkwrapped packaging, copying or otherwise using the SOFTWARE PRODUCT, you agree to be bound by the terms of this EULA. If you do not agree to the terms of this EULA, Gateway is unwilling to license the SOFTWARE PRODUCT to you. In such event, you may not use or copy the SOFTWARE PRODUCT, and you should promptly contact Gateway for instructions on returning it.

SOFTWARE PRODUCT LICENSE

The SOFTWARE PRODUCT is protected by copyright laws and international copyright treaties, as well as other intellectual property laws and treaties. The SOFTWARE PRODUCT is licensed, not sold.

1. **GRANT OF LICENSE.** This EULA grants you the following rights:
   - **Software**. If not already pre-installed, you may install and use one copy of the SOFTWARE PRODUCT on one Gateway COMPUTER, ("COMPUTER").
   - **Storage/Network Use**. You may also store or install a copy of the computer software portion of the SOFTWARE PRODUCT on the COMPUTER to allow your other computers to use the SOFTWARE PRODUCT over an internal network, and distribute the SOFTWARE PRODUCT to your other computers over an internal network. However, you must acquire and dedicate a license for the SOFTWARE PRODUCT for each computer on which the SOFTWARE PRODUCT is used or to which it is distributed. A license for the SOFTWARE PRODUCT may not be shared or used concurrently on different computers.
   - **Back-up Copy.** If Gateway has not included a back-up copy of the SOFTWARE PRODUCT with the COMPUTER, you may make a single back-up copy of the SOFTWARE PRODUCT. You may use the back-up copy solely for archival purposes.

2. **DESCRIPTION OF OTHER RIGHTS AND LIMITATIONS.**
   - **Limitations on Reverse Engineering, Decompilation and Disassembly**. You may not reverse engineer, decompile, or disassemble the SOFTWARE PRODUCT, except and only to the extent that such activity is expressly permitted by applicable law notwithstanding this limitation.
   - **Separation of Components.** The SOFTWARE PRODUCT is licensed as a single product. Its component parts and any upgrades may not be separated for use on more than one computer.
   - **Single COMPUTER.** The SOFTWARE PRODUCT is licensed with the COMPUTER as a single integrated product. The SOFTWARE PRODUCT may only be used with the COMPUTER.
   - **Rental.** You may not rent or lease the SOFTWARE PRODUCT.
   - **Software Transfer.** You may permanently transfer all of your rights under this EULA only as part of a sale or transfer of the COMPUTER, provided you retain no copies, you transfer all of the SOFTWARE PRODUCT (including all component parts, the media and printed materials, any upgrades, this EULA, and the Certificate(s) of Authenticity), if applicable, and the recipient agrees to the terms of this EULA. If the SOFTWARE PRODUCT is an upgrade, any transfer must include all prior versions of the SOFTWARE PRODUCT.
   - **Termination**. Without prejudice to any other rights, Gateway may terminate this EULA if you fail to comply with the terms and conditions of this EULA. In such event, you must destroy all copies of the SOFTWARE PRODUCT and all of its component parts.
   - **Language Version Selection.** Gateway may have elected to provide you with a selection of language versions for one or more of the Gateway software products licensed under this EULA. If the SOFTWARE PRODUCT is included in more than one language version, you are licensed to use only one of the language versions provided. As part of the setup process for the SOFTWARE PRODUCT you will be given a one-time option to select a language version. Upon selection, the language version selected by you will be set up on the COMPUTER, and the language version(s) not selected by you will be automatically and permanently deleted from the hard disk of the COMPUTER.

3. **COPYRIGHT.** All title and copyrights in and to the SOFTWARE PRODUCT (including but not limited to any images, photographs, animations, video, audio, music, text and "applets," incorporated into the SOFTWARE PRODUCT), the accompanying printed materials, and any copies of the SOFTWARE PRODUCT, are owned by Gateway or its licensors or suppliers. You may not copy the printed materials accompanying the SOFTWARE PRODUCT. All rights not specifically granted under this EULA are reserved by Gateway and its licensors or suppliers.

4. **DUAL-MEDIA SOFTWARE.** You may receive the SOFTWARE PRODUCT in more than one medium. Regardless of the type or size of medium you receive, you may use only one medium that is appropriate for the COMPUTER. You may not use or install the other medium on another COMPUTER. You may not loan, rent, lease, or otherwise transfer the other medium to another user, except as part of the permanent transfer (as provided above) of the SOFTWARE PRODUCT.

5. **PRODUCT SUPPORT.** Refer to the particular product's documentation for product support. Should you have any questions concerning this EULA, or if you desire to contact Gateway for any other reason, please refer to the address provided in the documentation for the COMPUTER.

6. **U.S. GOVERNMENT RESTRICTED RIGHTS.** The SOFTWARE PRODUCT and any accompanying documentation are and shall be deemed to be "commercial computer software" and "commercial computer software documentation," respectively, as defined in DFAR 252.227-7013 and as described in FAR 12.212. Any use, modification, reproduction, release, performance, display or disclosure of the SOFTWARE PRODUCT and any accompanying documentation by the United States Government shall be governed solely by the terms of this Agreement and shall be prohibited except to the extent expressly permitted by the terms of this Agreement.

7. **LIMITED WARRANTY.** Gateway warrants that the media on which the SOFTWARE PRODUCT is distributed is free from defects in materials and workmanship for a period of ninety (90) days from your receipt thereof. Your exclusive remedy in the event of any breach of the foregoing warranty shall be, at Gateway's sole option, either (a) a refund of the amount you paid for the SOFTWARE PRODUCT or (b) repair or replacement of such media, provided that you return the defective media to Gateway within ninety (90) days of your receipt thereof. The foregoing warranty shall be void if any defect in the media is a result of accident, abuse or misapplication. Any replacement media will be warranted as set forth above for the remainder of the original warranty period or thirty (30) days from your receipt of such replacement media, whichever is longer. EXCEPT AS EXPRESSLY SET FORTH HEREIN, GATEWAY, ITS SUPPLIERS OR LICENSORS HEREBY DISCLAIMS ALL WARRANTIES, EXPRESS, IMPLIED AND STATUTORY, IN CONNECTION WITH THE SOFTWARE PRODUCT AND ANY ACCOMPANYING DOCUMENTATION, INCLUDING WITHOUT LIMITATION THE IMPLIED WARRANTIES OF MERCHANTABILITY, NON-INFRINGEMENT OF THIRD-PARTY RIGHTS, AND FITNESS FOR A PARTICULAR PURPOSE.

8. **LIMITATION OF LIABILITY.** IN NO EVENT WILL GATEWAY, ITS SUPPLIERS OR LICENSORS, BE LIABLE FOR ANY INDIRECT, SPECIAL, INCIDENTAL, COVER OR CONSEQUENTIAL DAMAGES ARISING OUT OF THE USE OF OR INABILITY TO USE THE SOFTWARE PRODUCT, USER DOCUMENTATION OR RELATED TECHNICAL SUPPORT, INCLUDING WITHOUT LIMITATION, DAMAGES OR COSTS RELATING TO THE LOSS OF PROFITS, BUSINESS, GOODWILL, DATA OR COMPUTER PROGRAMS, EVEN IF ADVISED OF THE POSSIBILITY OF SUCH DAMAGES. IN NO EVENT WILL GATEWAY, ITS SUPPLIERS' OR LICENSORS' LIABILITY EXCEED THE AMOUNT PAID BY YOU FOR THE SOFTWARE PRODUCT. BECAUSE SOME JURISDICTIONS DO NOT ALLOW THE EXCLUSION OR LIMITATION OF LIABILITY FOR CONSEQUENTIAL OR INCIDENTAL DAMAGES, THE ABOVE LIMITATION MAY NOT APPLY TO YOU.

9. **Miscellaneous.** This Agreement is governed by the laws of the United States and the State of South Dakota, without reference to conflicts of law principles. The application of the United Nations Convention on Contracts for the International Sale of Goods is expressly excluded. This Agreement sets forth all rights for the user of the SOFTWARE PRODUCT and is the entire agreement between the parties. This Agreement supersedes any other communications with respect to the SOFTWARE PRODUCT and any associated documentation. This Agreement may not be modified except by a written addendum issued by a duly authorized representative of Gateway. No provision hereof shall be deemed waived unless such waiver shall be in writing and signed by Gateway or a duly authorized representative of Gateway. If any provision of this Agreement is held invalid, the remainder of this Agreement shall continue in full force and effect. The parties confirm that it is their wish that this Agreement has been written in the English language only.

"Rev.3 9/24/98".

Mission

To help everybody unlock the power of their computer to achieve their fullest personal, professional and lifestyle potential.

Deep inside one of America's leading computer companies you'll find a group of very smart, very dedicated people who have nothing to do with manufacturing computers.

With fresh insights and breakthrough techniques, the Survive & Thrive team is transforming the way we acquire technology skills. And putting a human face on the digital revolution. Yours.

Online Learning Subscription

Flexible and affordable, Online Learning gives unlimited access, anytime, anywhere. With one click, you get cutting-edge curriculum, message boards & online community.

Learning for your lifestyle

- Discover Digital Music and Photography
- Brush up your software skills
- Power your productivity

Start anytime - learn anywhere

www.LearnwithGateway.com

Learning Library

Delivering the benefits of classroom learning experience without the classroom, Gateway's Learning Library provides a step-by-step approach using powerful CD-ROMs to allow you to learn at your own pace, on your own schedule.

Offers include the following Learning Libraries:

- Microsoft Office XP Professional (Also in Spanish!)
- Microsoft Works Suite